Restored
Heart & Soul

Restored

Heart & Soul

By

Dave Bielecki

PRINTED IN THE UNITED STATES OF AMERICA

ISBN 978-0-9977727-0-8

Disclaimer: This book is a work of fiction. Names, characters, places, and incidents are products of the author's imagination or are used fictitiously. Any resemblance to actual persons, living or dead, is entirely coincidental.

To my father, Henry Bielecki,
who ignited my passion for Chrysler vehicles

Contents

Acknowledgements

Many thanks to Pastor Barry, and Ray, Jim, and Harriet from my church family, for their inspiration; to my wife, Diane, for her support; to the classic car community for all of their great classic car stories; to Wendy Scheuring for helping me write my story, and to Henderson Enterprises for editing and formatting my manuscript for publication.

Preface

I often hear people say that they would love to write a book but don't know where to start. The same thing happened to me. I had been ruminating about a story idea for years but had never acted upon it. Then last year, when a new pastor established himself in my church, he made it his mission to meet with each and every member to learn about their jobs, about their families, about what had brought them to God's house, and how they were faring on their spiritual journeys.

During one of my early conversations with Pastor Barry, I explained how I had been an Easter-Christmas Christian. I just made excuse after excuse about why I didn't need to attend services until my aunt Harriet became an integral force in bringing me back to the United Methodist Church where I have been a regular ever since. But, the one area where I felt I needed growth, I explained to Pastor Barry, was in witnessing to others.

Then, I shared with him the story idea that I had been mulling over. What if I wrote a book that shared a message of how God's love can restore hearts and souls?

The idea for this book first came to me when I began mowing grass at the church cemetery. There, I observed several men regularly visiting their deceased wives' gravesites. *Restored Heart & Soul* became a culmination of those experiences blended with my love of classic cars. All I needed was a nudge from Pastor Barry to take that first step in getting my story into print. I pray that you enjoy taking part in your own spiritual journey to a restored heart and soul.

God bless,
Dave Bielecki

Foreword

Life can be a journey, a road trip, or an adventure. The best way to live life is to decide that *God is now here* instead of *God is nowhere.* When we open our eyes, we will discover the reality of what Jesus promised: *"I am with you always."* It is my hope that, as you read this book, you will begin to see Jesus in your life and in the people and experiences around you. When you are hurting and need healing, look for that open church door, walk inside, spend some time to listen and pray, and you will soon discover that Jesus is in the restoration business.

~~Pastor Barry

"Come to me, all you who are weary and burdened, and I will give you rest. Take my yoke upon you and learn from me, for I am gentle and humble in heart, and you will find rest for your souls." Matthew 11:28-29 (NIV)

The Grave-Robber

The rhythmic sounds of the old man's shovel broke the still of the pre-dawn fog. The sun had not yet crested the eastern hills, and, along with the man, his secret remained shrouded in darkness. Before him stood a gaping hole next to a grey slate headstone that read:

ANNE MARIE JOHNSON //
1953 – 2011 //
Devoted Wife, Mother, Friend

Another foot to go, the old man thought to himself. "Honey, why do I feel like a grave-robber," he muttered aloud. The sound of his own voice was startling for it had been eerily quiet. *Maybe that's it,* he thought to himself as he began to dig again—this time, with a softer touch to make sure he didn't push too deep, piling each little bit of dirt on the back of the pile so it wouldn't slide back in.

He stuck his tape in the hole again and measured.

Nearly three feet.

He climbed down into the hole. Mist mixed with sweat dripped from the brim of his hat. He started probing around with a spoon.

CLINK.

It was the distinctive sound he'd been looking for—the dull sound of metal hitting thick marble, insulated by dirt. He dug with a spoon, then felt for the edge of the box with gloved fingers. He fell to his knees, grabbed the top edge and pulled, dislodging this treasure that had been buried for years.

"Finally, Anne. We're taking one last trip," he spoke softly.

Sunlight began to penetrate the early morning fog. He set down the box, picked up an extra bag of sand, and dumped it into the hole. He tossed in the old spoon and then shoveled the dirt pile to make an even spread. The light of dawn let him step back to appreciate his work.

"Can't even tell anyone has been here," he whispered approvingly to no one in particular. "Sure went back in faster than it came out."

He took off his dirty gloves and tucked them in his back pocket, carefully picked up his treasure, grabbed his shovel, and started the long walk to the van. It wasn't that far to the gate, but walking was painful as he limped slowly along.

"Well, shouldn't a grave-robber be fleeing for the getaway van?" came a voice from the cemetery shed.

The old man nearly jumped out of his coveralls, almost losing his grip on the box before he identified the voice as friendly. It was Larry, the cemetery groundskeeper.

"Sorry, Hank. Didn't mean to spook you," Larry added, realizing he'd just unintentionally startled his friend.

"This is it, Larry. I guess this is goodbye," Hank said as he looked at the blue box. He knew it was too late to change his mind.

"Hank, I am really going to miss you, friend. You're a good egg. But, I am also really happy for you."

Hank looked up. He couldn't explain it, but he suddenly felt better. He stood more upright, and looked at Larry squarely.

"I couldn't have done it without you, Larry," Hank spoke firmly, reaching out his hand.

The handshake was warm and firm but also comforting. There was an awkward silence.

"Well, this is...it, Larry," said Hank.

"Yep. I guess I better get mowing." *Same time, same day, same mow pattern.* Larry sighed as the mundane became reality once again.

Hank looked over his shoulder as he slowly ambled to the old van, adding, "I wish you had a remote control for that mower, Larry. Let it do the work while you sit by and watch."

He opened the front door and placed the blue marble box carefully on the passenger side, gently strapping it in with the seat belt.

"Kind of like old times. Huh, honey?"

After tossing the shovel, tape measure, and dirty gloves into the back, he hobbled to the driver's side and slid into the seat, backside first. The old van fired right up.

Hank glanced in his mirror as he started down the road. He saw Larry waving from the mower. Hank waved back, realizing it was the last time he would have his morning chats with Larry. No more bringing Anne red roses, her favorite flowers, either.

As he drove the long, winding gravel drive, Larry grew smaller and smaller in the rear view mirror. Hank hoped Larry saw him waving back. Finally, he and Anne were headed home.

The front end of the old van squeaked as Hank drove over the small bump into the drive. *Maybe I should grease that before we leave,* Hank thought as he parked and looked in the yard.

The yard looked good, neatly mowed. The FOR SALE sign was clean and neatly planted, not leaning over like Hank had seen in other yards. He got in the passenger side and took out his treasure, the marble box, and went inside.

The house was empty. Hank's footsteps echoed as he limped to the mantle to look at a framed picture of a woman in her twenties smiling, her dark eyes surrounded by her dark, shoulder-length hair.

Hank set the marble box down, lifted the top, and took out a ceramic urn with two red roses intertwined. Hank carefully set it beside her picture. Memories flooded through his mind, of how they used to dance, of how they talked when they were young...of how they talked before she passed.

Hank shook his shoulders. He needed to keep moving. No more time to sit and dream the hours away. He took one last look at those beautiful eyes which peered into his soul, just as they did so many years ago. "One more chapter to this story, Anne. The road trip you always wanted."

The Happy Daze Geezer Club

Most mornings, the parking lot of the Happy Daze Diner looked like it was hosting a classic muscle car show. A red '72 Chevelle, a customized '55 Sedan Delivery, a '70 chartreuse Mustang, a *Plum Crazy* 'Cuda, and a Pro-Street Chevy 3100 Pickup, among others, were meticulously parked in rows, neatly spaced, with a precise five feet between each car.

Today, a brand new 2015 white Camaro parked diagonally seemed a bit out of place, but not as much as the little blue Chevy S-10 which pulled in abruptly at 10:05 a.m. A weathered-looking old man hobbled out of the well-worn Chevy pickup he'd parked in his "assigned" space.

The bells on the diner glass door jingled announcing his entrance.

"Damn, Hank. What the hell happened to you," laughed Joe as he looked at his watch. "Tell me you got lucky last night. At least, that would be one of us." Everyone chuckled.

"Yeah, what's her name?" asked Hot Rod Tim peering from the latest issue of *Super Chevy Magazine*.

"Maybe there *was* a little hanky-panky going on last night," joked Shorty. "Looks like you can't even keep your eyes open."

Hank hated to admit it but he couldn't fool the members of the Old Geezer's Club, an eclectic group of Hank's old friends from the Chevy Car Club and his old church.

They knew Hank to be a little grumpy and mad at the world sometimes. Actually, a lot grumpy and mad at the world most of the time.

When he started this little social club at the diner, Hank had been a happy-go-lucky guy. But since the death of his beloved wife, Hank had grown cranky, tired, and angry. When he wasn't at the Happy Daze Diner or fixing up the house or doing yardwork, he could be found at Row 12, Plot 110 tending to her gravesite. Most mornings when the cemetery gates opened at 8 a.m., Hank visited her grave, talked to her about the latest car or truck one of the guys was working on, made sure to brush off her headstone of any newly cut grass, then drove straight to the diner for breakfast like clockwork.

Hank was a prisoner of routine, and to most outsiders, he looked like he had already died and been buried. His once vibrant smile had become a near-permanent frown. His face was bordered with frowning eyebrows and wrinkles.

But, the guys who knew him well also knew that beneath that hardened exterior, the "old" Hank, the church-going guy who helped his wife with the youth group, the guy who was accepting of everyone, the good listener who thought everyone's story was worth telling, had turned sour, blaming God for all of his pain. His friends were patient. They understood. Hank just needed some coaxing to come back out.

So, they bantered with him, figuring a few good jabs might bring a smile to his face. As usual, everybody was expecting the first words out of Hank's mouth to be some kind of complaint. Too much traffic on Main Street. Betty hadn't brought his coffee yet. Someone accidentally parked in his spot.

But, today, something was different.

He nodded to the three guys he had recently met at the cemetery, men like him, who didn't have much to do now that their wives had passed. They were the latest recruits of the Happy Daze Geezer Club.

"Jim, Bob, Ernic."

They all nodded back.

Hank pulled out a chair, sat at his same spot, the place where the two tables that were pulled together met.

"See this old Chevy Impala," said Bill as he paged through the *Super Chevy Magazine*. "Hey, I know you might not believe me, but I bought one like it back in '58. Ran the wheels off of her. Must have had more n' half o' million miles when I sold her."

"If you were a Ford man, you would've been lucky to get the odometer to roll over just once," said Mark. "Besides, Fords are so slow. If you ever owned one, you'd *still* be driving it today jus' trying to reach that milestone!"

"You don't know what you're talking about," said Shorty. "You're crazy, man. I've seen plenty of Fords that are still running after hitting that 500K mark. Fords rule."

"Well, I'll tell you what. You might be right, Shorty. I did see one of them little old church ladies driving her '66 Fairlane to service every year for the past 40 years. I suppose if you baby a Ford, it might last forever."

Dave Bielecki

"What's going on, guys?" asked Gary, who had just joined the group. He wore a clean pressed shirt with a nametag that read "Gary THE Auto Parts Guy".

"We were just asking Hank to spill the beans," said Joe, Hank's best friend.

"Is that right," said Gary. "Well, Hank..."

"Well...it's Kate. She's expecting...in March."

"When did you find out?" asked Joe.

"This morning. Three months along already."

"Hahaha. Grandpa Hank. Now, you're really old," Bill said as the guys all laughed aloud.

"You're going to have to start smiling now Hank. You don't want to make that baby cry every time it sees you."

"So, are you moving back east now?" asked Joe.

"To Baltimore? I couldn't do that. What about Anne?"

Jim, Bob, and Ernie from the cemetery all nodded in agreement.

Betty, the waitress, set a plate of two eggs over easy, Southern-style biscuits, and scrapple in front of Hank.

"Here ya go, Hank. Just like you like 'em. Now that you're all officially here, how's the baker's dozen doing this morning?"

Everyone watched as Hank took a bite. Just the other day, he yelled at Betty that the toast was too dark and told her to scrape the black off. "It's good. This diner's the only damn place in Kern County that serves decent scrapple. Just like they do back home."

"You mean Maryland? Well, if you're thinking that Maryland is home, it might do you some good to go back, Hank. I mean now that your family is growing," said Harry, whose wife Carol had been Anne's best friend.

"That Chevy pickup won't make it outside of the city limits," laughed Shorty. "You gotta go with a Ford, Hank."

Tim pulled out a parts supplier catalog from his jacket pocket in hopes of changing the subject. "Look, I just bought a new motor for my '67 Nova, and I'm sure to get the frame back from this old guy, Potter. He plans on having his old '32 High

Boy on the road in the spring. Everyone is welcome to lend a hand."

"A High Boy? Count me in," piped Shorty.

"I'm sure that Nova needs some new fenders too," said Gary, hoping that *deep pockets* Tim would spend some of his green at his auto parts store. "What's the interior like?"

"Pristine. Got it from an old widow."

"So what, are you guys trying to get rid of me or what?" Hank maneuvered the conversation back to himself.

"Uh, yeah, Hank. Of course we are," said Joe. "It's getting kind of crowded around here."

"Well, I don't know. Do you think Kate would...I don't know, do you think she'd want me to visit?"

Everybody got quiet. Hank pensively stared at his plate, coffee in hand, contemplating the possibilities. Without a word, every man at the table recognized that Hank had just taken an important step, even if that step was a small one. He had opened himself up to the idea of change, which made him seem not so much like a dead man anymore. Maybe, just maybe, Hank was considering rejoining the land of the living.

Making Plans, Moving On

Hank had been so focused on cleaning the fireplace that he didn't realize he was covered in soot when he was startled by the flapping of that pesky screen door. He stopped what he was doing, dusted himself off, and firmly wedged the screen door back into its warped wooden frame. The winds were picking up and the fall clouds were rolling in. As he turned back to his work on the fireplace, he got a hollow feeling in the pit of his stomach. This was a room that once roared with a warm, inviting fire. How many Christmases did he throw logs into that fireplace as he and Anne sat watching the embers burn 'til the wee hours of the morn. Oftentimes, he and Anne fell asleep in each other's arms as they discussed their plans for the coming year.

One particular year, six Christmases ago, they both had decided to buy an old 1969 Dodge Sportsman window van, just like the one they had in college. It had the engine between the seats and a small galley right behind the driver's seat with an ice box and a small stove and sink. There was also a small sofa in the rear that could be converted into a bed.

Yes, it was a little outdated and, yes, it needed a little tender loving care, but they decided to buy it, rip out the interior, and make it more modern, more comfortable. They laughed as they talked about how they would go on a road trip to parts unknown like New Mexico or Arizona, maybe even see the Grand Canyon or cruise along Route 66. To Hank, it still felt like yesterday they had been making those plans.

The wooden floors in the living room still creaked in the same places, and all of Anne's knickknacks were precisely as she had left them on the L-shaped coffee table. The afghan she had crocheted him in college was still thrown over the back of the rocking chair he built for her. But that once warm, inviting room now felt cold and dark and gray.

On the mantel, next to Anne's smiling photo, was a picture of Kate wearing a blue winter snowsuit in front of a three-foot snow drift. There was a picture of Kate on her 18th birthday, too, just before she went to college back in Maryland. How she had her mother's eyes and smile. He reclined on the sofa for a moment, forgetting he was dusted in soot, to reflect on all he had lost. A beautiful wife. A vivacious daughter. The house so silent now that not even memories of Anne's smile could warm it.

And Kate. She had been such an energetic child, always running, playing, getting bumped and bruised, always full of life. He remembered how happy he and Anne had been when they first held that little bundle of life. She had always been Daddy's little girl, but after they moved to Bakersfield, she had grown distant, preferring the company of her friends. Hank silently reverted to working on his cars or the house and somehow forgot how to talk with his daughter, Anne becoming the conduit between the two. He hadn't seen Kate since Anne's funeral. Kate sometimes called, but their conversations felt awkward and stilted. As the days slowed for Hank, so did the calls become infrequent. But, a few days ago, Kate made a surprise call that changed Hank's life.

"Dad?" It sounded like Anne's voice on the line.

Hank remembered how the phone rang and how he almost didn't pick up. "Hello?"

"Dad? Dad, how are you?"

"Oh, I'm fine here, Kate. How are you? It's been a long time."

"Well, Dad, I know. I'm sorry. It's just that...well...I just thought I should tell you the news."

That news made his heart skip a beat. It felt something like joy. He hadn't felt that way in a long time. Anne would have been so happy. Just thinking about it now brought a tear to his eye. He decided to go back to his soot and his cleaning and the fireplace. Then, that darn screen door slammed again.

"So, Hank. Are you going to sit around here and mope some more, or take my advice and move closer to your family?" Joe made himself at home, plopped himself on the sofa, letting that annoying screen door slap shut behind him.

"Joe, when did you get here?"

"Well, you *were* deep in thought," he smiled. "So, have you thought about what I said?"

"About going back to Maryland? Gosh, Joe. I don't know. I mean me and Kate..."

"Anne's been gone for five years now, Hank. You need to accept that and move on, buddy. You should go live by family."

Joe, himself, had been divorced for 15 years and spent his life raising his son, J.R., who was now in his twenties. He was a devoted family man, with the family that he had left.

"I know that Kate called me to tell me the good news, but now in thinking about it, I kind of have cold feet. I just don't know if she's forgiven me."

"There's only one way to find out, Hank. Go be there when your grandchild is born. It will give you both a new beginning. Babies have a way of doing that."

"I have to admit, ever since she called, I feel different."

Hank still had his doubts. *Would Kate want him there? Should he just go visit? Move there? Sell the house? That would be impossible. There was just too much work.*

"When Patty left me, it was a kick in my gut. But, I had to get over it, Hank. I had to...for J.R."

"Yep, and now J.R. is 20-somethin' years old. You did a good job raising him. He's a fine young man. Now, let's talk about something more interesting. What's going on with you and that Judy?"

"That's what I wanted to talk to you about."

"It better be good."

"Well, there's good news and there's bad news."

"Spill it."

"Well, Judy was named most successful realtor in her office. She's doing great. But she's so busy selling houses, well, that doesn't leave much time for a relationship. But, I'll be waiting around for when she slows down. A woman needs to go out to dinner, no?" Joe said. "Anyway, I thought she'd be perfect for what I have in mind."

"And, what would that be?"

"Hank, she could sell your house in a jiffy. She'll get you the best deal on it. Trust me. She is one smart woman. She'll sell this house in no time."

Sell the house? Move to Maryland? Become a grandfather? Funny how life can change in only one day.

"Okay. I'll think about it," Hank muttered under his breath.

Joe pulled his cell phone out of his shirt pocket, flipped it open, looking right at Hank. He typed a quick text, hit SEND, and closed the phone.

"Judy will be here in two minutes," he said as he slipped the flip phone back into his pocket. "You're gonna love Judy, Hank."

There was a quiet pause. Hank started to change his mind. *Maybe this is too fast. I need to think about...*

Hank's thoughts were interrupted as Judy pulled into the driveway, got out of her sedan, and glided gracefully through the front door.

"This is great news, Hank," exclaimed Judy.

"Wow, that was fast," said Hank perking up a bit.

"Well, you know how Joe is." She cast him a smile, giving Joe an indication that maybe he shouldn't write her off, just yet. "I'd be happy to help you, Hank."

Hank's mind was swirling with so many thoughts that he just stood there dumbfounded while Judy was busy glancing around.

"If it's too overwhelming, I can come back at a later time," she said sweetly. Hank could see why

Joe was so attracted to her. Professional. Well-spoken. She had a genuine kindness to her voice.

"Well, since you're here. What do you think?"

"If you don't mind, I'll have a look around?" she asked pointing to the staircase. Hank gave her the go-ahead to work her assessment.

"Joe, you can't let this woman go," Hank whispered once Judy was out of range. "She's perfect for you. Attractive. Nice dresser. A real go-getter."

Joe raised his eyebrows in agreement. The men chatted a bit until Judy came back into the room.

"Hank, this place is in immaculate condition! There are just a few things to do. For starters, I think we need to fix this screen door. And then after that I think we should stage the house," Judy said.

"You mean make a production of it?"

"That means we have to get rid of the clutter, put out your best furniture, make the rooms look more spacious, welcoming, inviting," she said. "What do you think?"

Hank nodded.

"And there's one other thing," she said. "We've *got* to do the same thing to your garage—DEE-CLUTTER! All those boxes and garbage bags, everything inside has to go. Tell you what, let's have a garage sale Saturday morning. Will that work for you?"

"Yes, Ma'am," Hank said. Joe winked at Hank as he watched Judy walk out the door. She exuded such confidence and professionalism that Hank felt he was in good hands.

"One day, that gal is going to be mine," Joe said. "I just need to be patient."

The next Saturday rolled around. When Hank pulled in from his usual cemetery visit, he had completely forgotten about the yard sale. *His yard sale!* As he pulled into the driveway, he saw Judy, Joe, J.R., Carol—Anne's best friend—and some of the neighbors milling around.

"Hi Hank," smiled Judy. "How are you?" Hank could see that a lot of his stuff, household appliances, books, knickknacks were set out neatly on tables.

"What the heck were you doing in this garage, Hank? Hoarding junk for a rainy day?" Joe slapped him on the back in jest, but Hank looked down at the ground. He was embarrassed. Those bags were full of Anne's stuff, things she had asked him to get rid of years ago. But, he just couldn't part with any of it.

"Oh, hi Mr. Johnson," said the kid from next door. He was holding Anne's old desk lamp.

"Oh, I remember that lamp. Anne used it in college. She used to study by that lamp. Did I tell you she had straight A's in Chemistry? She was such a smart bird. What about books? I've got some of Anne's college textbooks, dictionaries. Maybe you need a desk? Why I remember when Anne…"

"Uh, that's nice sir, but how much is the lamp?"

"Three dollars," Carol smiled.

"Okay, sold," said the young man as he walked off with the lamp.

"I don't know if I can say this kindly, Hank," Judy said, "so I'll just say it. This packrat persona just doesn't suit you. You need to change your mindset from packrat to *benefactor*."

Judy was a genius. In one simple sentence, she'd completely disarmed all of Hank's excuses for getting rid of junk. Hank knew he had been procrastinating. He had never thought of himself as a packrat. But, *benefactor?* He liked the sound of that.

"Well, one man's junk is another man's treasure, right?" Hank added.

"After the garage sale, a few friends and I will take what's left to charity," offered Carol.

"Yeah, and J.R. is going to haul what's left after that to the dump," Joe added. "By the way, Judy has already scheduled your first showing next week."

What? A possible buyer? First they haul out all of Anne's stuff and now the house is practically sold? "That was fast," Hank said wiping the sweat off of his forehead.

"I told you she was good, didn't I?" said Joe with a grin.

"They are a cash buyer and they're looking to move in in thirty days," Judy added, having overheard the conversation. "But let's not call it a done deal until they come over to see the place."

Things were moving way too fast for Hank. Way too fast.

After the sale, when the neighbors and the junk and the things stuffed in garbage bags had been taken away, Hank looked into the garage. There it was. The old van. Sure, that old custom paint job had seen better days. One of the tires was completely flat. But still, if someone were looking for a good solid vehicle to restore, this would be the one. As one of the guys from the old car club used to say, "She ain't too hateful."

"I can have J.R. list it on eBay for you," said Joe.

"eBay? Really?"

"Yeah, he's always on there, looking for cars. They sell everything. I'll have him wash it. Take some nice photos. Surely it should be worth a few thousand. That's if it still runs. It still runs, doesn't it?"

"I guess now's the time to find out."

Hank hopped in, tapped the gas pedal twice, and turned the key. A little clatter-tapping down under the frame. Again, and the same thing.

J.R. pulled Joe's car up and popped the hood. Joe hooked the jumpers. Hank tried and again, the same tapping.

"Well, it's either the battery or the starter," Joe surmised. "We'll never push this van out with that flat. J.R., let's get a rope and pull her out."

They hooked a rope to the bumper and pulled it into the driveway, a classic van for all the world to see.

"Don't worry, Hank. We'll get her started. Remember that guy named Potter I was telling you about the other day? He can probably fix her up for you."

They said a few more words, small talk mainly, then Joe and J.R. left with the last of the junk.

Hank looked at the empty garage and the empty yard. So much emptiness. The only "fun" part of today had been the few minutes trying to solve the van-in-garage problem. What a relief he felt when the fellas left. It felt good to be alone, in that comfortable place where he had resided for years. Now it was just him and his broom.

But as Hank started pushing that broom, rhythmically sweeping the years of dust and leaves away, his lips turned upward, revealing the beginnings of a smile.

Chicken Man to the Rescue

"All clear!" Joe hollered as he motioned to Hank to try one more time.

"It's no use," Hank said as he turned the ignition and heard the familiar click of a dead battery. After checking the solenoid and points and everything else they could think of, Hank relented. "It's just not going to start. We should probably give your buddy Potter a call."

"Yeah, I guess I was hoping we could save him a trip and you a tow." Joe reached for his phone, dialed Potter, and let the phone ring at least ten times.

"Hey, Potter. We're going to need you to give us a tow. That's right. 76 Amber Lane. See you in twenty." Joe slapped his phone shut. "He's on his way."

"Well, why don't we get her cleaned up before he gets here?" suggested Hank.

"Yeah, I'm dying to figure out what the original color is," Joe laughed as he turned on the faucet and hosed off the van.

"It was groovy green," laughed Hank. "But, Ann wanted to repaint it 'hippie-style'. Something she called a...a rainbow motif, I think."

"Oh, that would have gone over well," laughed Joe. "Two old hippie artists in a rainbow love van heading to the Grand Canyon."

"I can think of worse things," Hank smiled inwardly as he looked up from washing the rear window. Joe was crouching over, fervently scrubbing the front hubcap.

"What's the problem, Joe? This Potter never seen a little dirt before?"

"You don't know Potter," Joe said. "Anything we can do to help him be a little less cranky will go a long way. He hates making house calls. This guy's an artist when it comes to working on cars, though. That's how he got his name, 'Potter'. Seriously".

"You mean his name's not Potter?"

"This guy's a legend, man. Real old school. Some say his hands are blessed, like a Potter with a wheel," Joe paused, his gaze indicating he was somewhere else. "He can mold anything into a masterpiece. I've seen it with my own eyes."

Joe snapped back and started working his way around to the rear passenger side of the van. "That's why I asked him to work on your van. This guy can work miracles. If you've got a mechanical problem, he can fix it. No matter what."

Hank continued to scrub the back of the van. "I think she's ready for a rinse now."

"Potter started working on cars during the golden age of drag racing back in the early '60s," Joe paused as he traveled back through time. "Those were the days, man, when there was no substitute for horsepower. Potter didn't believe in fancy turbochargers or fuel injection systems. He had invented his own bag of tricks for making these cars mean machines. He could rebuild a carburetor in his sleep, change gears in a rear end in minutes. He just knew every inch of these old rides. Back in the day, if you wanted to be on the winning side of the track, Potter was your guy. His custom body work rivaled famous car designers of the day, but without all the fanfare."

"Sounds like the kind of guy I want working on my van," Hank said.

"Yep. For Potter, it's all about the cars."

After they hosed her off, the van looked pretty good, Hank thought. They finished just as Potter pulled into the driveway...in a battered 1957 Chevy 3100.

"And, you were worried what he was going to think about *my* van?" Hank muttered to Joe.

Potter pulled up matter-of-factly, popped open the door, and took his time getting out of the truck, real methodical-like. He extended an oily hand to Joe.

"Hey, Joe. Is this the hunk-o-junk you wanted to waste your money on towing back to my shop?" Potter snorted.

"The name's Potter." He nodded in Hank's direction.

"So, I heard," said Hank.

Potter's tow truck looked like it had just driven off of the set of that Pixar cartoon movie, *Cars*. The guy looked like a cartoon character himself, thought Hank. And, in thinking how some say that people can resemble animals, this guy looked like a chicken. Potter's wrinkly skin was a bit yellowed, and when his grease-smeared cap fell off, his slicked over red hair resembled a rooster's comb. The big nose added to the entire package. Hank had to fight the urge to call out, "Hey, Chicken Man!"

"Here, you try," said Joe as he threw Potter the van keys. Potter got into the seat and made a few half-hearted attempts to get the old gal going, then he looked at Joe and just shrugged his shoulders.

"So, what are you going to do with this old hippie van?" Potter barked at Hank out the window.

Old sin bins, thought Potter. *I'll never figure out why these old hippies get so attached to these pieces of junk. Even the junkyard's too good for 'em.*

"Well, we were hoping you'll fix her up," said Joe.

"It's gonna be one hundred to tow her back to the shop then," he said with his back to them as he made his way to his truck.

"But, it's only five miles down the road."

Joe motioned the throat-cut sign to Hank as he pulled out a wad of cash and put it on the dash of the Chevy.

Hank and Joe watched as the slow wench on the wrecker lifted the van's back wheels off of the ground, which had been as painful as dealing with Potter himself. After the van was secured on the truck, Hank felt nostalgic as the old Chevy pulled her out of the driveway.

It was a darn shame that the old van's first voyage after years of hibernation was behind that old tow truck, Hank thought, *but at least she'll be getting a second chance.*

The next morning, just after he got back home from the cemetery, Hank got a phone call from Potter who summoned him to his shop. Immediately.

Potter's shop was in an old section of town. On the outside, it was dirty and unorganized and looked out-of-place, like it fell out of a '50s car magazine. But the inside was different. Hank was mesmerized by the vintage muscle cars and other old classics in various stages of restoration.

A '52 Mercury, which had been turned into a "lead sled" years ago, was up on a lift. Its bright yellow paint job made the whole shop light up. Two Chevys on the lot out back—'64 and '66 Impalas—probably cost so much to restore that the owners must have cashed out their retirement accounts to have Potter put his special touch on them. Those Chevys would have taken first and second place in any car show. Hank was sure of that.

I wished I would have known about this place years ago when my neighbor wanted to sell me his '69 Plymouth Road Runner, thought Hank. *Bet Potter could have turned her into a show winner.*

Hank's old Dodge stood out among the cool cars in the small, tidy lot. Parked between the two Chevys, Hank's old Dodge seemed to have a frown on its grill. When Hank walked into the shop, Potter jumped out of his creaky old wooden desk chair in his out-of-the-way cubby-hole office, leaving most of his lunch on the cluttered desk. He motioned to Hank with a fried chicken leg in his hand as he led him outside to the van, pointing out to Hank all the work that needed to be done under the hood. The good news was that he got her running, but there were some electrical problems from it sitting in the garage all those years. Potter shouted out the remaining needs in rapid-fire sequence: Some rewiring, four tires, fluid changes, brakes, shocks, battery, muffler, and a couple of spot-welds. The total would be around $1,500.

"If I were you, I'd junk the old thing. Damn hippie van."

"Well, I'd like to fix it...for sentimental reasons," Hank explained. *If the old gal only sold for $3,000, I'd still make $1,500.*

"Fine," Potter said as he took a bite out of the chicken leg. He was anxious to get back to his lunch and then to getting that damn old hippie van off his lot as soon as possible.

Joe owes me on this one, Potter thought.

"It'll be ready the day after tomorrow."

Two days later, when Joe brought Hank to pick up the van, they were amazed. The old van looked like it had had a face lift. She started right up and sounded almost like she was purring, like she was years younger and happier, too.

"Thanks, Potter," said Hank as he swiped his credit card. "How can I ever repay you?" Hank felt truly thankful and appreciative of Potter's role in making his and Anne's dream of restoring the old van come true. "Why don't I treat you to breakfast? Joe and I are heading to the Happy Daze."

"Can't eat none of that mess at the old greasy spoon. I got a figure to maintain."

It was the first time Hank had seen ole Potter smile. And that was that. Hank would probably never see him again. And, frankly, Hank was okay with it.

As Hank drove into the parking lot at the Happy Daze Diner, the old geezers were all outside waiting for him. Hank could barely get out of the door before the guys put their two cents in.

"If I remember right, my family used to have one just like it. Sorry to say that they sure were glad to get rid of that piece of crap," Ernie said wryly.

"Too bad it doesn't have a Chevy Bow Tie on the front," laughed Mark.

"Hey Hank. Since you put so much into it already, why not just hold on to it? You are in way too deep now," joked Shorty.

"I thought they crushed all these things way back in the Nixon years. How did this sorry sack miss its date with the crusher?" chuckled Harry.

The jokes continued to roll about the van, but Hank didn't let any of them get under his skin. He actually started to laugh along with them. Life was good. And, even the old van looked happier today.

After breakfast, Hank drove the van home and J.R. took some pictures and listed it on eBay. Hank even decided to park it out front with a FOR SALE sign.

"I used to have one just like it," said Ned the mailman as he drove up to Hank's box that morning.

"Are you interested in buying it then?" Hank asked.

"Hell, no. Hated them back when they were new," he chortled.

And that's how it went for the first week. It seemed as if the old Dodge could not get any love or respect. Even the neighbors hinted that he should park it back in the garage.

But, on the eighth day, J.R. called to say that he had received a bite on the ad. Turned out a prospective buyer from Baltimore offered $1,000 but couldn't afford the shipping expenses.

"Dear Sir," the email said.

I would give anything to have this van. It is exactly like the one that my dad owned. My dad has since passed away, and I'd like to honor my dad by buying this van and fixing it up in time for his van club's 40th anniversary.

Thank you, Dan

Hank decided not to respond to the email and let the listing expire. J.R. relisted it but with the same results. No one local was interested in buying it. Actually no one was interested in buying it, except for Dan—the same guy from back east—who emailed again. Go figure. And so, Hank decided to write back.

Dan,

After keeping the van all of these years, I would like it to go to someone who would love it and restore it back to its glory days. My wife and I had a van just like it when we were in college. When we found this little jewel six years ago, we were planning on fixing it up and taking a road trip out west somewhere. Suffice it to say, that never happened. But, I'd be interested in knowing what plans you have for it if you were to buy it.

Looking forward to your response,

Hank

Dear Hank,

Well, first of all, I've got to tell you why this van is *The One*. Out here on the east coast, everything rusts. But yours, even though it needs a paint job, looks great. I can work with it. I want to restore it, to get it to look just like the one my dad had. Down to the same colors. He had a lot of great times with his buddies in that van. I can't repeat all the stories he used to tell me about all the shenanigans they did. Let me just say that he had such a great time that my mom hated it with a passion. She often said, "I hated that stupid van club," which is putting it mildly. But, don't worry about her. That was a long time ago. I know she wouldn't mind me working on the van in the garage. I just really would love to have the van. It would mean everything to me and the guys in the club.

Sincerely,

Dan

Hank emailed Dan and asked him to call. During their conversation, Hank detected the sincerity and passion the kid had for restoring the old van. Hank knew that giving Dan the van would make Anne happy. And, that their dreams would be realized through the young man. It was a done deal. Paperwork completed. Payment on its way. Still, there were details to work out.

"Joe, I'm in a fix," Hank sounded the alarm as Joe answered the phone.

"Now what, Hank?"

"Remember the van?"

"How could I forget it?"

"I sold it on eBay."

"I know. J.R. told me. How are you going to get it to Baltimore?"

"That's why I was calling you."

"Uh-huh?"

"I'm thinking about transporting the van back east. I can haul my stuff in a U-Haul with my truck. Once I get to Baltimore, I can sell the truck and buy something new. But..."

"Yeah?"

"Do you know of anyone that can transport the van out east at a reasonable cost?"

"That piece of junk?" Joe let out a belly laugh. "No, but I do know a guy who has space left on his big box truck that can take out your stuff. Why don't you sell off your truck here and make that road trip you always wanted in the van?"

"It just wouldn't be the same without Anne," Hank lamented. "But, what if..."

"What?"

"Well, J.R. could probably use a commission for selling my old truck, right?" Hank asked, his mind already made up. "I'll give him twenty percent of whatever you get for it."

"Aw, Hank. We couldn't."

"Yes, you could. You've been a great friend and J.R. is a great kid." *Be a benefactor.* Hank recalled Judy's wise words of advice.

"Well, in that case, okay. You've convinced me."

It was a done deal. Hank hung up the phone and immediately dialed Potter.

"Hey Potter, you remember the Dodge van you fixed up for me a few weeks ago?"

"That piece of junk? I'm still trying to forget I put my hands on that thing."

"Well, all that aside. How roadworthy do you think it is? I mean, do you think it can make it cross-country?"

"That van? Oh yeah, it's as sturdy as a tank."

Things were suddenly falling into place. "Well, thanks Potter."

Potter slammed the phone back on the receiver. "Damn hippie Van. Probably won't make it out of the state."

Restored Heart & Soul

Goodbye, Beloved Anne

Well, this is it.

Hank felt the gravity of what *it* really meant. This would be his final visit to the cemetery, to Anne's final resting place. It would be his last "goodbye" to the only tangible, touchable piece of Anne he had left.

"Dammit!"

The sudden sound of that word stumbling out of his mouth echoed through the near-empty house. The last time he used a curse word like that was when Anne's sister Barb had Anne's urn buried in a plot at Riverside Cemetery. Years before Anne had even become ill, Hank and Anne had decided they wanted their ashes to be scattered on the Chesapeake Bay, near the shore where they had met.

"Well, that felt kind of good," Hank spoke aloud to no one. It felt real. It felt cathartic.

But then the mental debates returned again. The ones that had been torturing him the past several days, and sleepless nights.

Maybe I can still back out. What if I declined payment for the van? What if I told Judy I had a change of mind on the house? Could we refund their earnest money? I could get my furniture out of the storage pod. No problem. But, what about Kate?

Hank grabbed his keys, started out the door, revved up the truck, all while watching movies not yet filmed in his mind: Meeting Kate and her husband for the first time in a long time. Holding *his* grandbaby! Rocking her to sleep. Reading her a bedtime story. Taking her fishing . . . *That's what Anne would want, wouldn't she?*

As he neared the cemetery, Hank realized that Anne wasn't the only one he was leaving. There was the band of cemetery "regulars" who'd gathered nearly every morning after paying their respects. The guys at the diner. There was Larry, too. He had forgotten about Larry.

Larry was the Riverside cemetery caretaker, and a man who had been a big part of Hank's life almost every day for the past five years. Hank liked Larry. Heck, most everybody who knew Larry liked Larry, and the more people got to know him, the more they liked him. Larry performed his groundskeeping job to perfection.

But while the old men who would gather regularly at the cemetery appreciated and sometimes thanked him for his dedication, it was Larry's heart and mind that made him so likeable.

Hank thought that Larry had certainly missed his calling. Folks were amazed how Larry could solve anyone's problem. He was an idea man. He was also a counselor, a pastor of sorts, a psychiatrist, and a coach. He solved personal problems, career problems, financial problems, even technical problems. The shared opinion among Bob, Ernie, and Jim—Hank's friends from the cemetery—was that Larry's mind wasn't choked by the minutiae of life. That's what freed him to come up with brilliant solutions to pretty much anything.

Hank recalled a time when he and some of the guys were trying to console Bob, a "newcomer" at the cemetery. Larry had seen the men congregating near a mound of dirt covered with flowers marking a new gravesite. Larry hopped off his mower to see how things were going for the new widower.

"Really tough," Bob squeezed out between nose-blows and wiping his eyes. "Really tough."

"What's the matter, buddy?" Larry asked.

"Louise's medical bills are more than I can pay. The damn buzzards are calling every day. Even at night!" Bob went on. "They said they are going to foreclose on our house if I can't pay. And I live on Social Security and a little pension and I can't pay any more than I am."

Hank could empathize with Bob's tale of financial woe. Anne had passed five years ago, and he was still paying off her medical expenses.

Larry had a unique ability to build a rapport with others, to really hear what people were saying. There was something calming about the way he spoke, too. It was a gift, and all the fellas who were regulars there knew it.

"Let me think about it, Bob," Larry said, patting Bob on the shoulder as he got back on his mower. And off he rode, mowing his perfectly straight lines between gravesites.

Bob somehow seemed to recover, so much so that he changed the subject. "Do you guys think the Dodgers will make it all the way this year?" he asked the guys. Then, they all started talking.

When Larry finished his rounds, he parked his mower and walked over to the small group of men, exuding a contagious energy.

"Ok, they can't take your house, Bob," Larry explained without missing a beat. "Your house is protected. In fact, I read that it's illegal for them to even threaten your domicile! So, if they say anything like that again, tell them you're going to report them. That'll stop that nonsense."

Larry paused, then continued. "Next, if you pay *something* you can afford every month, they can't really take *any* action against you. In fact, you can even stop the harassment!"

Everybody in the group was amazed. How could a groundskeeper be so knowledgeable about so many things?

Hank, still on autopilot, woke up from his daydreaming and drove through the wrought iron gates that marked the entrance to the cemetery. There was Larry. Riding his mower like always. Hank waved as Larry made his turn. Larry smiled and pointed at his watch, noting that Hank was 15 minutes later than his usual time.

Hank got out of the truck and slowly labored to Anne's plot. He set down a small bunch of flowers he'd bought the previous night. He picked up the old ones and put them in a bag. He stood up. Straightened his shirt a little.

"Well, this is it, Anne." Hank spoke softly. He looked around her plot and tried to take everything in. He wanted to remember. "I know you would want me to go see Kate. I wish..." Hank paused. He breathed in deeply. The smell of fresh-cut grass filled his nostrils. The sound of Larry's mower hummed in the distance.

Am I doing the right thing? If this is what Anne would want, what everybody thinks is best for me to do, then...then why does it feel so wrong? Why is this wrenching my soul?

"Anne, I don't know if I can do this. I want to see Kate and take that trip...but...but leaving you behind...is just killing me."

Larry was on a long straightaway watching Hank talking to himself and gesturing. When he pulled up behind Hank, he stopped and shut off the mower and hopped off. "Well, Hank. Rumor on the street is you got some news."

Hank turned around. "I do. I guess I'm moving."

"Moving on?"

"Well, yes and no," Hank said, looking down, shifting his weight off his sore leg. "Kate's having a baby, and I got the van sold and road-worthy and..."

"What?" Larry interrupted. "Kate's having a baby? You're going to be 'Grandpa Hank'? That's great news. And you're moving? Amen!"

"Well, sorry I didn't tell you sooner. Everything just seemed to happen so fast. Like everything just fell into place: The house, yard sale, truck, van..." Hank stopped mid-sentence. "You know, I never planned to bury Anne's ashes, Larry."

"I know," Larry said changing his tone and putting his hand on Hank's shoulder. "I know."

"I...I...I just hate to leave her."

There was a long pause. The sound of a dog barking in the far distance broke the silence.

"Larry, when Anne and I talked about it long ago, we...we agreed that we were going to have our ashes spread over the Chesapeake. That's where we first met, you know?"

"Well, Hank. I got some thinking to do," Larry said as he started towards his mower. Hank knew what 'thinking' meant—mowing was Larry's "thinking time".

"It'll be my cookie break in a few. Don't get away without saying bye, Hank."

"Wouldn't think of it, Larry."

Hank sat on the hard marble bench near Anne's plot to wait for Larry. He looked out and saw some of the other guys. Jim was doing his usual manicuring of his wife's site. Hank remembered when Larry told Jim that he needed to lighten up a bit so he wouldn't put him out of a job.

It seemed to Hank like only a few minutes had passed when Larry walked up with his bag of cookies. Larry said a short prayer. Hank bowed his head, but his mind was on Larry's cookies more than his prayer. Almost before he finished the "Amen," Larry started, "While I was mowing, I got this idea, Hank."

"Uh-huh?" Hank nodded as he grabbed a cookie.

"Yeah. Well, you have a problem, right? You're torn between leaving Anne's remains here while you take the trip you'd both planned together, right?"

"Well, yeah. I guess that pretty much sums up my problem. But, not much I can do about it now. I mean, I can't really back out. And if you're going to suggest I come back and visit, I was hoping to do that, but..."

"Yeah." Larry looked at Hank squarely.

Larry slid close and put his arm around Hank and they bent forward, changing the arrangement from leisurely man-talk into a huddle.

"I think I have a solution to your quandary, Hank," Larry began. He spoke in hushed tones, but his excitement was amplified by the occasional squeezes of his fingers on Hank's neck. And like Lombardi detailing some plan for victory, down by two scores at the end of the fourth quarter, Larry unfolded a plan that just lifted the burden from Hank's heart, untied the knot in his gut. Hank breathed out a long wind, and leaned back against the bench seat. A songbird warbled.

"Larry, you, my friend, are a genius." Hank was floored. "You really...?" Hank stopped mid-sentence.

Larry grinned. Nothing more needed to be said. "Thanks, Larry. Thank you."

As soon as Hank got home, he called Joe right away.

"Hey Joe, Hank. Hey, I've got some all-the-works pizza pie from Mimi's coming around five and some cold specialty beers and some good news, all with yours and J.R.'s names on it, if you wanna stop…"

"We're there Hank!" Joe interrupted. "We'll see you at 5. I don't know what it is you're about to share, but I can feel it through the phone. I might have to come early!"

"See you at five. Ciao."

"Ciao? Did you say 'ciao', Hank?" That *ciao* was not Hank, but even Hank wasn't acting like Hank.

If it were possible for a man to smile toe-to-crown, Hank was smiling from the bottoms of his shoes to the top of his head. That night, when the pizza delivery guy came, Hank opened his wallet and pulled out an extra $20 bill as a tip.

This ought to surprise him, Hank grinned, realizing that when it came to tipping, he had been even worse than Scrooge.

It was going to be a great night!

The Last Supper

"I'm leaving first thing in the morning, Joe," Hank said as he pulled out one of the folding chairs to take a seat at the card table.

Joe spit a pizza-beer concoction out of his mouth. "What the heck, Hank."

"You can't expect Judy to consider even going out to dinner with you when you talk with your mouth open, Joe," Hank joked. "And, not only that, we need to man up and thank the Lord for what we have."

"Seriously?" asked J.R. who had never known Hank to utter a prayerful word out of his mouth, let alone confess himself to be a believer.

Joe shot his son a disdainful glance.

"Yes, seriously," Hank paused. "Let's take a moment to thank the Lord for what we've got." Before he could get a consensus, he closed his eyes and lowered his head in prayer.

"Dear Lord. Thank You for my friends. I ask for a special blessing for J.R. and Joe. They have helped me so much. But, most of all, I thank You that everything has all come together. Kate, the baby, the house, my belongings, even the old van. I'll no longer worry about a thing. I know, Lord, that You will always work everything out for the good."

"And, for protection for Hank on his cross-country journey," Joe piped in. "In a crusty old van. Although it's a little sooner than I had expected. I thought I had another week with the old fart." Joe fought to keep those blasted tears from coming out of his eyes.

"And, thank You for this pizza, and especially for the beer," added J.R.

"In Jesus's name. Amen," Hank ended.

As the three men gathered together for one last time in Hank's small kitchen, Hank couldn't have thought of a better way for he, Joe, and J.R. to share their last supper together.

Between mouthfuls of Mimi's pizza and cold beer, Hank filled them in on his plan to leave in the morning, right after breakfast at the Happy Daze, to say goodbye to the guys, of course.

"Why are you in such a hurry? You've got another week until the new owner moves in. We haven't even sold the pickup!" argued Joe.

"Yeah, Uncle Hank. How much do you want me to sell her for?"

"J.R.'s got the truck covered," reassured Hank. "Don't you J.R.? You know what it's worth. I trust you will do her right. Don't worry, Joe."

Then Hank filled them in on his neat little plan to "take" Anne with him to Maryland. He told them all the details. How he'd get to the cemetery before sunup, how he'd retrieve his precious Anne, and cover his tracks all before the cemetery opened. And, that Larry was the mastermind who had concocted the whole scheme. They all nodded in agreement that this Larry fellow was certainly a genius.

"Not only that, Joe, Larry gave me clarity," added Hank. "I now feel I can finally move on with my life."

"Well, I have to admit it. I'm a little jealous of Larry's ingenuity. Wish I would've come up with that plan myself." Joe smiled as he opened another beer. "Hey Hankster, remember that time when you and I were bidding on that '69 Chevy Camaro? Hah. I will never forget that look on your face when I won. That was a classic moment, wasn't it?"

"Yeah, if it wasn't for that fist fight, we would still be buddies today," laughed Hank, as he let loose and slugged a beer, recalling how in the past, that auction had always been a sore spot for him. "But, you fixed her up like a beauty. I couldn't have done it better myself."

"Well, I do have to give ole Potter *some* of the credit."

"She sure shined at that Desert Classic Car Show. Won first place, right?"

"Yeah, that was a great day," said Joe. "If it wasn't for her, I wouldn't have the Camaro I have today. She was the first in a long line of babes. Too bad those babes were all cars."

"Remember Charlie from the car club?" asked Hank. "He made your friend Potter look like a kindergartner, didn't he?"

"Yeah, that guy worked one classic after another. Remember that lime green Mustang? She was certainly a lady, wasn't she?"

"Did he ever show you the engine?"

"Damn. Yes. Like it had never been driven."

"Damn shame what happened to him."

"Who was Charlie?" asked J.R.

"Man, Mimi's still got it going," Joe said as he grabbed another slice of pizza. "You know, I still remember those home cooked meals that Anne made when my dad passed. Now that woman could cook."

Hank paused a moment. Anne was such a thoughtful woman. Always helping. Always reaching out. He still hurt inside from missing her.

I wonder if she would she be happy I'm taking her along on this road trip, Hank thought.

"Aunt Anne's hamburgers were the best. So was her apple pie," said J.R., filling in the uneasy silence.

"You sure all systems are go with the van?" asked Joe.

"Roger. Potter assured me she's a cross-country girl."

Joe's phone buzzed. His eyes lit up when he saw it was Judy. "Hi Judy. I'm here at Hank's place. Seems he's leaving ahead of schedule."

Joe smiled in Hank's direction, giving him the *thumbs-up* sign. "Great. Super, Judy. Thanks so much."

"You don't have a thing to worry about, Hank," Joe said as he flipped his phone shut. "Super-Agent Judy has everything under control. You are good to go. You've got your walking papers."

"Thanks, Joe. Well, even if I didn't, I think I'd leave anyway. The time is right. I need to get the hell out of Dodge."

"Don't think you're going to do a disappearing act. I'm not too set in my ways to not just hop on a plane and pay you a visit. You aren't getting rid of Joe McFarlane that easily," he said as he slapped Hank on the back.

When the men all said goodnight, Hank sat at the card table for a few minutes and gave the living room one last glance. He remembered one particular New Year's Eve. Anne snuggled up on the couch asleep. Kate heading out to a New Year's Eve party. Hank told her to drive carefully. And to be home before 1 a.m. She rolled her eyes at him, kissed him, and went out the door.

The house was now still. Hank closed his eyes and tried to sense Anne's presence. But, he couldn't. All he could hear was the quiet creaking of the steps as he slowly climbed to their bedroom to sleep in their house one last time.

At 4:46 a.m., Hank shut off the alarm before it would begin its blaring. Hank had been awake most of the night laying in silence, thinking about the long road before him. He washed his face, combed his hair, put on some clothes, and hurried down the steps, locking the door, never looking back. He had a date with Anne to keep.

Restored Heart & Soul

New Beginnings

After Hank pulled into the parking lot of the Happy Daze Diner, he took a moment to reflect. This would be the last time he would see all the guys together. He realized what a great group they had been, and he suddenly felt remorseful about his past behavior. These guys were *real* friends. And now, Hank had made the decision to venture back to his hometown without even knowing if any of his old friends were still around, and if they were, would they even want to rekindle the friendship? He would have his daughter and his son-in-law. But, they wouldn't be like the guys. And, what if Kate and Matt didn't have time for him? Or, if his grandchild didn't like him?

Joe honked his horn and motioned for Hank and J.R. to hurry up. J.R. had been sitting in Hank's Chevy S-10, with his hands drumming the steering wheel, radio turned up, mouthing the words to some '80s classic song.

Hank looked at the marble box as it sat silently on the passenger seat. "Honey," he whispered. "Are you sure this is what you want me to do? Give up my friends? Friends I haven't always treated well, but who accept me for who I am?

Friends who haven't left me, even though I've been acting like a jerk? How many times have I complained to Betty about the food or the coffee or the service, and she never got mad? That girl deserves a raise."

Joe honked again.

As Hank lumbered out of the van, Joe remarked, "What's wrong, buddy? You having second thoughts?" J.R. jumped out of the truck and smoothed his hand over the hood of the Chevy.

"No," said Hank resolutely. "I'm having thoughts, but not second thoughts."

Joe and J.R. followed Hank as he entered the Happy Daze Diner for the last time. J.R. picked up the local car shopper magazine from the adjacent rack. He sure wished he had the money to buy Uncle Hank's truck. First thing he'd do would give it a new paint job. Maybe blue. Just like the original. Maybe he'd get a few flames painted on it, too. That would be cool. He'd get that classic steering wheel he had seen in a car parts magazine, and some of those custom wheels he had been drooling over. He'd soup up that old girl to 300 HP and tear through town. Uncle Hank wouldn't even recognize her.

"Hey, J.R. Come on," said Joe. "You got your head in the clouds? The guys are waiting."

J.R. put the magazine under his arm and headed toward the table with a bunch of old guys sitting around yacking and laughing.

"Hey, Junior. You can sit here," said Bill as he jumped up and grabbed a chair from a neighboring table. "What ya got there? Some good reading material?"

"Yeah. Sure do," J.R. said as he extended a hand. "Trying to get a price on Uncle Hank's truck. My name's J.R."

"Oh, that's easy. You can ask anyone here. Everyone except for Shorty, that is," joked Bill. "The name's Bill."

"Hey kid, you might want to put that magazine down and come to a real parts store," laughed Gary. "We're having a sale tomorrow."

Betty glided to the table with her usual smile and brought two menus, one for Joe and one for J.R.

"I need a menu too, Betty," said Hank. "Please."

"What? No two eggs over easy with a biscuit and scrapple today?" Betty asked with surprise in her voice. "Well, Hank. If you say so. I'll be right back with that menu. Young man, take your time. We have some delicious fixings to choose from."

"I heard you're leaving today?" Jim blurted out.

Hank looked at his watch. "In about 45 minutes. That's if the service is dependable," he said winking at Betty as she poured Hank's coffee.

"I just gotta say," said Ernie. "If it wasn't for Hank here, me and Bob and Jim, we wouldn't have met such a great group of guys. Thanks for inviting us, Hank."

"Amen. Couldn't be a nicer group of guys," said Bob. "We've had some great laughs. Been good for the soul."

"I'll third that," said Jim. "If we wouldn't have met Hank, we'd still be keeping company at the cemetery."

Hank waved Betty back over to the table. "Uh hum. How about you guys? Ready to order?"

Betty came around with the coffee and topped off everyone's cup. "What'll it be, Hank? My, I never thought I'd ever say those words."

"I'll take the western omelet," said Hank, and he slapped the menu shut.

"I'll take a stack of pancakes with extra butter. And a double order of bacon. Got any of those fancy syrups to go along with it?" asked J.R.

Betty nodded. "Maple, blueberry, strawberry, boysenberry."

"I'll take the blueberry. Oh yeah, and some sausage, too."

"Got it. And, you Joe?"

"I'll take the veggie omelet," said Joe under his breath. The table was doused in laughter. "Too much pizza and beer last night . . . at Hank's," Joe confessed. The guys mercilessly slapped the table chuckling and yacking.

"You didn't have any ladies over there last night now did you?" joked Tim.

"Oh, I was there chaperoning," said J.R. dryly.

"This kid's pretty funny. I say we make J.R. here a junior member of the Old Geezer Club," said Bill. "We've got an empty seat to fill now."

"I second that."

"Let's call him Hank Junior."

"Hank Junior? One Hank is enough for me. Let's just call him Junior," laughed Shorty.

"Junior it is," said Hot Rod Tim. "But, we gotta fill you in a little bit. You've got some big shoes to fill."

"So, you see, Junior, you think *you're* eating a lot? About 15 years back, I went to this potluck dinner at the truck club and I see Hank piling every dish in the place on his plate, like he hadn't eaten in ages," said Bill. "He was the only guy eating like me and I says to him, I says, 'Are you trying to bulk up like Charles Atlas or something?'"

Then, the laughter died down, and the talk got more serious.

"So Hank. What's your plan?" asked Gary.

"Well, today, I'm going to take 58 to the border then catch I-40."

"That's it? At that rate, you'll never get there," barked Shorty. "Damn Dodge. See what I mean?"

"What's Kate think about all this?" asked Harry.

"Oh, so you're planning on taking the ole Route 66?" quipped Bill.

"You forgot. He sleeps at the wheel," said Harry. "Remember the time that you and Anne and me and Carol were driving back from Lake Tahoe?"

"She said she's looking forward to me coming out there to visit," answered Hank. "I'll probably stay at a little motel or two along the way, and sleep in the van some of the nights to save some money." He told them he'd probably like a shower every other day anyway.

"To visit? You mean, she doesn't know you're coming out there for good?" asked Mark.

Betty brought Joe's veggie omelet, a huge stack of pancakes with bacon and sausage for J.R., and Hank's western omelet.

Hank stared at his breakfast. The huge omelet was practically hanging over the plate. She topped off Hank's coffee.

"Hank probably forgot to tell her that little detail," laughed Joe. "But, everything always works out for the good. That's what I say."

As those words rolled off of Joe's tongue, Hank realized he had made the right decision. *Everything always works for the good.* "Betty, this is the best damn coffee I've ever had. What did you do?"

"It's the same coffee I've been serving for the past seven years, Hank. But today, I think your taste buds are different," Betty said with a smile as she walked back to the kitchen.

"Hey, Hank," Harry shouted out. "I can take that truck off of your hands. How much you want for it?"

"Sorry. It's sold."

"Hey Uncle Hank, I thought you wanted me to sell it for you. I just found one in the car shopper just like it, figured out a good price for you, and am ready to put an online auction posting up this week. What's up?"

"Forgot to tell you, J.R. Your dad and I already found a new owner."

"Oh. Because I was going to try and find some way to buy it from you," mumbled J.R.

"Hey kid. I mean, Junior," said Hot Rod Tim. "I got a fixer-upper you can buy real cheap. What do you say?"

"Please tell me it's a Ford," said Shorty.

"Thanks for your offer, but it just wouldn't be the same." J.R. didn't just want a Chevy S-10, he wanted *that* Chevy S-10. He had spent his growing up years with Dad and Uncle Hank in *that* truck, listening to their stories, about their past cars, about their lives.

"Hey kid, wipe that ugly look off your face and take a look at the back of the title," said Joe.

J.R. opened the white envelope and saw his name on the section where the new owner's name goes. There it was in bold, black ink. After 25 long years, the vehicle was finally changing hands, and those hands were his. A big grin was plastered across his face.

Betty came over to top off Hank's coffee once more, but Hank waved his hand. She just had to see what that grin was about.

"Hey Betty," said Bill as he whipped out his cell phone. "Go stand behind Hank there. I'm gonna take a group shot." The guys all gathered around, and then Betty switched places with Bill so they all could have a picture of the original baker's dozen, plus one.

Sam, the cook, bolted through the kitchen door carrying a huge chocolate sheet cake to the table that read, "Happy Trails, Hank." Hank was speechless; and for a moment, the diner became still and quiet until Bill started to sing, *"For he's a jolly good fellow..."* and the others joined in.

They all ate cake and joked around a bit more and then one by one, the guys took turns saying goodbye to Hank. They shook hands and hugged and said their goodbyes again until Joe and J.R. were the last ones left. J.R. hugged Hank and said, "Thanks so much, Uncle Hank. I'll fix her up. Make you proud."

"I know you will, J.R. Take care of your dad for me. Make sure he doesn't get into any trouble."

"I will," J.R. said and then the two best friends were left alone. Betty came by to wish him well.

"Hank, I don't think I'll ever have another customer like you," she said as she gave him a hug. "Be good now," she said as she walked away.

"Well, Hank. It's just you and me," said Joe as they slowly walked out of the Happy Daze Diner together. "I don't know what to say, except I'll be seeing you soon."

"Thank you, Joe...for everything." The two old friends hugged and then Joe patted Hank on the back for old time's sake. Neither of them wanted to shed a tear in front of the other, but those tears were there all the same.

Restored Heart & Soul

East-Bound and Down, Good Buddy

As the van rambled down Route 58, a cool breeze blustered in from the windows. Hank, sleeves rolled up, hair waved back, radio on, was thankful that he'd put Anne's ashes in the built-in ice box. Potter could have done better with the shocks, he thought, feeling every bump in the road in his body, but it was a brilliant October morning, and he couldn't complain. He was glad he was able to leave a couple of weeks earlier so he could dodge the snowbirds flocking to Arizona.

There it was. The Bakersfield city limit.

He caught a glimpse of what? A blue Chevy in the rearview mirror? It was a young guy with wavy dark hair. J.R.? Maybe he had left something at the diner? He slowed to get a closer look, but it wasn't a Chevy.

"Well, this is it then. Goodbye Bakersfield." The California story had come to a close. "Thanks for everything. It's been a good ride."

A text message chimed in. "Must be Joe checking up on me. Who else could it be?" Everyone else had given up on texting Hank because he never texted back.

As Route 58 headed toward the mountains, Hank felt as if he were going to drive right into the monolith. Something about the mountains comforted his spirit. With Anne by his side, he and the van had a 2600-mile commitment to keep. He drove past the little mountain towns of Keene, Walong, Cable, Golden Hills, Tehachapi, known for its famous 360-degree train track that looped around the entire mountain.

Now that would be quite a ride!

Nearing Mojave, Hank entered high desert territory. It was arid, dry, raw, and brown. He passed Edwards Air Force Base, and the little towns of Silt, Rich, and Boron, with not much in between. Sometimes the temperature gauge on the van would read a little high, but then fall back to normal. He began to worry. What if he broke down in the desert, ran out of gas, or got a flat? Would anyone be able to help?

Mile marker by mile marker clipped by and, with them, a slight ennui. The heat emanated from the black tar in waves; the dips in the road looked like black lava lakes. He pulled off into a little town called Kramer Junction, with its massive solar fields, to take a break. As he pulled off the exit ramp, he saw a young woman about Kate's age holding a baby flagging someone down. A white F-150 stopped and picked them up. Hank decided to pull into a gas station to read the text message that came in.

Dad. Still coming to visit? Matt and I are going to D.C. this weekend. Call me. I have my cell.

"Hey Mister," a young guy with a ponytail yelled as he ran out of the decrepit-looking station. "You need gas? We're out but I've got a few gallons in the back. That should hold you to Barstow."

"About how far?"

"'Bout half hour."

"No, I'll make it. Keep the gas for someone who needs it. Thanks, though."

"Okay, Mister. You sure? That's a really cool van you got there."

Hank nodded and got back on the road. As the highway traversed through mountainous sand dunes, he was amazed at how massive the Mojave Desert was.

In Barstow, Hank grabbed a cup of coffee at the local diner, gassed up, and texted Joe. *Almost to State Line. Tell the guys they lost the bet. LOL.*

"You know what, Annie? I'll even surprise Mr. Joe and send him a picture of where I end up tonight," Hank said with a laugh.

As he continued east, Hank switched the radio to a country station. One of those catchy tunes was playing. Country music always tells some kind of story. This song was about two strangers, a man and woman drinking at some bar, arguing about whose ex was worse.

"Annie, why in the hell do some people get divorced? Maybe if they had what we had, it wouldn't happen. Yeah, we argued a little bit about you and Barb and how *sisterly* she was, as you call it. But, you know, she was a bit of a trouble maker, stirring up the pot when it didn't need any watchin'. She even buried you without asking me, Annie, so I didn't even tell her about our little plan. And you know what, Annie? People don't try anymore. They just give up. You don't really know what you've got until you lose it, Annie. You know?"

The radio announcer interrupted Hank's monologue to interview the lead singer of some hometown country band playing gigs along Route 66. They called themselves the Lonely Ramblers. It sounded like a lame name to Hank, but it also sounded like they were picking up quite a following. People hopped from bar to bar trailing them along their stops and the crowds were growing with each stop they made. They'd be playing at the Cactus Bar in Barstow tonight.

Guess they're not so lonely anymore, Hank thought to himself.

He changed the station and found himself singing along to that old Eagle's song about a girl in a Ford. Tomorrow, he'd probably be in Winslow, he thought. Maybe he'd stop by just to see that famous corner.

Maybe a girl would drive by in a flatbed Ford. Heck, Shorty would love that.

He continued singing with the static until he drove out of range and forgot the rest of the words. The miles spun under the old Dodge's wheels, a car or two here or there, a blue desert sky, 85 degrees, dry air, and a sense of nothingness.

Route 66. Maybe he should turn off of the interstate and take it for a while. Listen to that country band, maybe get a beer, and find someone to dance with and what? Anne was here and he was thinking about having a night on the town? He put his focus back on the road passing the desert towns of Ludlow, Fenner, and Goffs. Places that no one knew even existed.

Those towns could get swallowed up in a sand dune and no one would ever know, Hank thought.

Needles. 10 miles. Finally, greenery. The Colorado River streamed through the town, dotted with houses on its shores. *Goodbye California.* The highway dipped south then northward again passing through desert mountain chains and a town called Yucca.

"Annie, remember when you wanted me to try that Yucca stew you made and I said no way? I'm sorry about that, Annie. I'm sure it was pretty good. Hah! Speaking of food..." Hank reached into Judy's care package and grabbed a bottle of water and a can of Pringles. "This here's good eatin', honey. What do you say?"

He passed a little town called Kingman, and figured he'd better find a place to bed down for the night. All he saw were mountains and desert and more mountains. Crunching the chips kept him awake, but he sure wished he had a cup of coffee. Then about ten miles down the road, he saw a beacon of light, a sign that read *Welcome to the town of Run Amok, AZ.* "Yep, this will be home for the night. Joe is gonna love the name of this town."

He pulled into a gas station to fill up the van, paid an additional quarter a gallon to get premium, and checked the coolant. As he walked into the station, the bell on the door was so clamorous that he got an instant headache. He "woke up" the few "customers" that the place had. They all gave him one of those "you ain't from around here" looks.

"Any good eatin' around here?" Hank asked.

"Eden? Sorry, mister," a short man with long, black hair said with a thick accent.

"Restaurants. You know, places to eat?"

He directed the question to the workers who were "on break".

"Well, you're pretty far from Eden. In fact, I'd say you're at the other end of the stick. You're lucky that we're on break, Pops, to answer your questions 'cause we have nothing else better to do," said an enormous man wearing an oil-stained work shirt with a nametag that said "Kenny".

Hank looked around and saw that this place definitely wasn't hopping. A fellow even larger than Kenny got up from his stool.

"So you need a good place to eat and somewhere to crash for the night? The name's Big Ray."

Big Ray looked like he could tip the scales at 450.

"Me and Kenny kind of like the all-you-can-eat spot just a mile up the road. You can't go wrong at Bertha's Buffet, but we won't be able to join ya. We've been banned for a few months," Big Ray grinned as he pointed to his apparent eating partner, Kenny.

"The only camping place in town is behind the buffet. That sort of makes it good. You can just roll downhill to your site after fillin' yourself up. Don't forget to try all six types of gravy, and your own six pack of rolls to mop it up," laughed Kenny.

"Thanks, guys," said Hank. "I'll look into it," he said under his breath.

As Hank drove further, the flickering lights decorating a quaint little diner caught his attention. "Looks like a better bet than that buffet." The sign, painted bright blue and yellow, read "Daisy's Diner". He ordered a burger and fries and a Coke, ate quickly, and decided to bed down for the night in the parking lot.

"Probably shouldn't sleep here. There's a mobile home park a few blocks from where I live if you're looking to find somewhere to sleep," said a waitress who just finished her shift for the night. "Ain't too bad and they welcome overnighters, I think. Just don't have modern facilities."

"Why thank you, ma'am."

As Hank pulled into Little Hurtin' Campgrounds, it looked more like a trailer park, with one corner set aside for RVs and Campers. It wasn't his first choice, staying at a place he judged to be seedy and probably full of troubled folks, but he was too tired to care.

Hank pulled up to the office to register when an old guy, as rude as W.C. Fields, practically accosted the manager.

"I saw kids. What are kids doing here? Do I have to go to another RV Park?"

"Clint," scolded the manager, "Those are Gerry's grandkids. Just visiting. They'll be out before lights out."

Hank figured out that this was a 55+ adult park, and this fellow was taking things way too seriously.

The manager looked at Hank with an "I'm sorry" kind of expression and told him he could register in the morning.

Once the kids left, Hank expected the seedy trailer park hermits to let loose with drinking, swearing, and carousing. But all lights were out, and it was as quiet as the desert. Maybe they were all inside drinking the night away. It was okay with him as long as he could get some sleep.

The next morning, Hank was alarmed when he looked at his watch and saw it was 9 a.m. How could he have slept in so late? This would definitely put him behind schedule.

The manager stopped by and brought him a bottle of water. She made some small talk, mentioned she moved here when she divorced because it was cheap.

"Divorces are expensive," she said. "I was a loyal wife to my ex for 12 years. That was until the relationship got a little crowded if you know what I mean. Still, I stayed to see if we could work things out. Wanted to try on forgiveness. Not my strongest suit. Still, I thought we could fix things up. We were going to counseling, but I couldn't trust him anymore. I don't know why I'm going on and on about this with a stranger. Guess I'm not over it yet."

Hank nodded sympathetically.

"Most of the residents here are like me." She pointed to a homemade sign demarking a little dirt road that said "Divorce Court." Jojo's husband used to beat her so bad her face looked like a prune, but she was afraid to leave him. Turns out, he ended up in jail and now she's free, but he wiped out all of their savings. She's got a job waitressing at the diner."

"That's incredibly sad," said Hank.

"Yeah. And, it's not only the womenfolk. Todd's wife was cuckolding him with the Postmaster next county up. She moved out one day when he was at work and cleaned out the whole house, and there was nothing he could do about it. Seems like you just can't trust anyone anymore."

Hank took another look at the trailer park. It was a community of hurting souls. No wonder they called it the "Little Hurtin' Campground." In the daylight, it didn't look quite as seedy as he thought it did last night. "How much do I owe you for the night?" he asked the manager.

"You a church-going man? If so, just put a little extra in the plate," she said. "If not, just try to help out someone along the way."

"Well, thank you, ma'am," Hank said as he tipped his hat in her direction. "I certainly will."

Hank's stomach was growling and his heart couldn't take any more tales of woe. All he was thinking about was how good it would be to fill his belly with some hot cakes, sausage, and eggs from the Daisy Diner, but now he didn't have time. He needed to get on the road. Pronto.

He turned the key. Nothing. Again. Nothing. "Damn, I left the parking lights on," Hank muttered dejectedly as he shut the lights completely off, something he would have done if he hadn't been so exhausted when he parked. He got out of the van and slammed the door in frustration.

"I got a battery charger in the shed, but no jumper cables. Bet we have you up and going within the hour," a voice said from behind.

A tall, frail-looking man stood behind him. "We can charge your car while you have some breakfast. Want to come in?"

Old Charlie's mobile home was real old and rustic smelling, kind of like a construction site office trailer. He kept it tidy, though, and neat. Very homey. Kind of like Rockford's place in that old '70s TV show! Hank hoped no one would hook up the trailer and haul it away while they ate.

"You live here alone?" Hank asked.

"Yes, sir. My wife passed away years ago. I'll never stop loving her, but I can't keep thinking about what I don't have. What's past is past."

Hank nodded as he spooned some scrambled eggs into his mouth.

"Ketchup?"

"No, thanks."

"It hit me real bad in the beginning. She got hit by a car while she was stopped at a stop sign on our own street. I couldn't work. Couldn't eat. Couldn't sleep. I couldn't drive down our street without thinking about the accident. Darn well lost everything I had. Then one day I walked into this church to go to grief counseling. Never looked back."

Hank told him about his road trip adventure with Anne, how he stole her remains and was going to take them to their final resting place on the Chesapeake Bay.

"It's probably time."

They walked down the rickety steps to check on the van. Hank turned the key, put his foot on the gas, and it started right up.

"I don't know what to say. At least let me pay for the meal," Hank said.

"That's okay, Sonny. Just pay it forward."

"Thank you, Charlie," said Hank, not knowing what to say. "You're a real friend."

These small acts of kindness kindled his spirit. Before he headed onto the interstate, he stopped by the Daisy Diner with the van still running, ordered a quick cup of coffee to go, and left an anonymous tip for Jojo.

He spent the day singing to the radio, talking to Anne, and stopping to take his picture in Winslow to send to Joe sans girl in flatbed truck. After a stop to view the deep reds of the Petrified Forest National Park, he found a small lodge just at the state line where he could get a shower. As he lay on the bed with Anne's ashes beside him, he looked at his phone and saw that Joe had texted him ten times, asking him if he was okay, that he was worried, and to call him.

"Yeah, sure. Don't be such a worrywart, Joe," Hank texted but it didn't send. He tried again. No coverage.

Hank clicked on the television news and saw a report that nearly 200 cars and trucks had been buried in a mudslide the day before on Route 58, just east of Mojave, California. Pictures of jack-knifed trucks and mud-buried cars and rescue operations flashed across the screen. Just two days ago, he had been there. He silently said a prayer for those affected. If he had any second thoughts of going back to Bakersfield, that road was now closed.

Don't underestimate Hank, he texted Joe on his phone. *New Mexico State Line.* He'd hit the SEND button tomorrow.

Today Is Your Lucky Day

"Today's gonna be a great day!" Hank said aloud. He took a deep breath of crisp mountain air and said a small prayer of thanks that he had made it this far.

He grabbed a coffee from The Donut Shack and continued his journey. It was only two and one-half hours to Albuquerque, and he would get something to eat there. He'd send that text to Joe when he got into the city, too. And, then there was the problem of Kate. He needed to tell her he was coming home for more than just a visit.

The highway climbed into the mountains, and Hank was enjoying the change of scenery. He started singing the lyrics to that Partridge Family song about Albuquerque. He had always liked the tune but never admitted it to anyone.

If only the guys could see me now. They'd be doubled over in laughter. But, what the heck. The lyrics are good, and I've just rediscovered my singer self!

When Hank made it to Albuquerque, he stopped at little local restaurant and ordered the carne adovada. "Red or Green?" The waitress asked.

"How about Christmas?" Hank said feeling adventurous.

After lunch, his plan was to find a truck stop near Amarillo and sleep for the night. He passed the little towns of Moriarty and Clines Corners, then came upon the exit for 84 North.

"Annie, wouldn't it be fun to drop some slots in Vegas? That's one place I never took you. Should have. But, you know me. I was never a risktaker. Always the straight and narrow guy, but I was pretty narrow-minded if you ask me. Forgive me, Annie."

He spent the next hour ruminating about the *could-haves* and the *should-haves* and the *wish he would-haves.*

Shoot! He had forgotten to send that text to Joe! He'd try again when he got to Amarillo. Which reminded him that he needed to start thinking about what he was going to text Kate.

Maybe I should text something like:

"I'm in New Mexico. On my way to Maryland. Making pretty good time. Looking forward to seeing you."

No. Too formal. Not like a note from a father to daughter.

"Kate, I'll give you a call. I'm on my way to Maryland. I've sold the house and am planning on staying a while."

No. Too drastic.

"Dear Kate. How are you? To answer your question..."

That's just plain stupid.

"Heading to Maryland. Planning on staying. For a while. Love, Dad."

Yep, that's it. I'll text that when I get to . . .

Grrrtch!

The engine seemed to seize, and Hank coasted to the berm. He jumped out of the van, and lifted the hood.

"This is *not* good!" Hank could feel the heat radiating from the engine. There was oil leaking and coolant spewing out. "Damn, Potter. '*She's sturdy as a tank.*' Right."

Standing in the mountain breeze, Hank felt a little bite to the air, and he was starting to feel cold.

"You'd think only a few hours outside of Albuquerque there'd be more traffic than this," he muttered. "We're smack in the middle of Nowhere, USA, Annie."

A car appeared and Hank watched intently, hoping. It was a middle-aged lady, but she didn't even slow down.

Hank checked his phone—no coverage. He realized that Tucumcari was at least 20 miles in the other direction. He stood by the driver's side, hoping someone might show some goodwill and stop.

About an hour later, a State Trooper pulled up behind the old van and parked. He got out and looked at the engine with Hank.

"Doesn't look like your van's in a good way, sir. I know someone who can help you. There's a tow trucker, a real good guy, about 15 miles up the road. Let me call Dispatch and we'll get him up here."

I sure hope that this really *good guy isn't gonna be anything like Potter. Then again, finding someone out here to get the van fixed and back on the road isn't going to be easy.*

Hank realized he wasn't in any position to be choosy. He just hoped it was something simple. And cheap.

"Dispatch says Lucky will be here within the hour. You'll be okay?"

"Yes. Thanks, officer. I'll be fine."

An hour later, the flashing lights of the tow truck illuminated the early evening sky. Hank could hear the roaring diesel engine make its way down the mountain. It made a wide U-turn, stopped, and a tall, skinny man hopped out.

Today is your Lucky Day, the sign on the truck door said.

"I sure as heck hope so. Better not cost a fortune either," Hank mumbled. The truck wasn't brand new, but at least it was made in the 21st century. It looked tough enough to handle the job, much better than Potter's sorry excuse of a tow truck. It was a roll back, which swiftly winched the van up onto the bed.

"My name's Clyde, but you can call me Lucky. Everyone else in town does. You can stay in the van on my lot 'til I get to it," Lucky offered as he made a tight turn on the mountain highway heading back to his shop. "Might save you some money."

"Mmm hmmm," said Hank. "That's nice of ya."

"There's a cord you can plug your stuff into, like if you need to charge your phone or shave or something. My nephew Jimmy keeps the restrooms pretty clean. He can check on you every day when he comes by to feed and water the cats."

"Every day? How long do you think this is gonna take?"

"I'll have a look in the morning and I'll let you know."

When they pulled up to Lucky's Super Service Center, it was pitch dark, except for a paltry, flickering light on the sign.

Whatever. Hank was too tired to worry about anything. He just resigned to crashing in the van tonight and to let tomorrow take care of itself.

Eight a.m. sharp, Lucky was pounding on the van window.

"Hank, come take a spot on one of those chairs," Lucky boomed with way too much energy for this early in the morning. "Today's your Lucky Day, partner. There's some fresh coffee in the office if you'd like some. Jimmy made it. Strong enough to grow you a five o'clock shadow."

With that, Lucky was checking under the hood.

Hank opened the van door and covered his eyes from the brightness of the morning sun. As he walked towards the office, the sign outside the front office caught his eye: *Lucky's Super Service Center* bordered by two real horseshoes. Only the outskirts of the town were visible from Lucky's, but from what Hank could see, it looked like the town came out of the '60s.

Hank worried about how much the repair was going to cost. That kid Dan didn't have money for an expensive repair. But, it wasn't Dan's idea that Hank take a cross-country road trip either. Still, Hank was saving Dan money by driving it to Maryland rather than having it shipped.

Maybe I should ask him to go half and half on the repair bill, thought Hank.

Hank watched Lucky and Jimmy push the van into the bay. Lucky started his investigation, but kept getting interrupted with small repairs, fixing flats, responding to calls from the State Police to take gas to stranded motorists. After several hours, Hank started to see that Lucky was doing everything *except* diagnosing his van.

Finally, around evening time, and after hours of interruptions, Lucky pushed the van back onto the lot and motioned for Hank to come into the office.

"Threw a rod, buddy."

Hank knew what that meant. The engine was toast.

"Now, I'm more of a Chevy guy," Lucky said real slow-like. "Don't know much about them Mopars, but I'll do good by you, buddy."

Hank had to tilt his head to look up at Lucky who stood about a foot taller than he. "For some reason, I believe you will," Hank said.

And so, Hank began a waiting game, his fate completely in the hands of Lucky's ability to find a sound used or rebuilt engine to replace the blown engine. Every day was nearly the same:

Hank living in the van without air conditioning during the warm days, and no heat in the cool evenings.

On the second night, feeling rather parched, Hank woke up to get a drink. He was met by a rather large and hairy tarantula living in his sink.

Maybe he's thirsty, too, thought Hank. *As long as he stays on his side of the Dodge, no problem. I can use a little companionship.* "You look like a Fred," Hank told the tarantula. "That's it. I'll call you Fred."

During the days, Hank passed the time watching cars speed by, talking to himself, and hanging out with the cats that roamed Lucky's shop. He mostly ate beef jerky and single-serving soups from Judy's care package. And, there was Lucky's vending machine, which he was cleaning out of chips and candy bars.

By the fourth day, a county Sherriff vehicle showed up on the scene, and Hank wondered if he had come to arrest Lucky for bad business practices.

"Hello, Deputy. I'm certainly happy I got the tow the other day to Lucky's. But, I must say, I'm losing faith in 'ole Lucky. Progress on getting my vehicle fixed has come to a halt."

The Sherriff's Deputy looked at Hank long and hard. "Lucky is good people. He even asked me to bring you a few sandwiches." He handed Hank a bag, got back in into his Tahoe, and drove off.

That was odd, Hank thought. *Maybe Lucky and the lawmen in these parts have some kind of racket, and he can run his shop more like a hobby than a business. Lucky seems to love towing cars, but unless they're a Chevy classic like that old '67 Malibu in the extra bay, he sure doesn't seem particularly interested in working on any.*

The next morning, with Lucky nowhere to be found, Hank told Jimmy in frustration, "If my damn van were a GM, maybe he'd put his heart into fixing my engine."

Lucky's nephew, Jimmy, ran a search of local junkyards and found what looked like a promising replacement engine. "I'll tell Uncle Lucky about it. That's all I can say."

That afternoon, to pass the time, Hank grabbed a broom and tidied up a bit. He found a yellowed Chamber of Commerce pamphlet in Lucky's "reading materials" rack and read that Bella

Vista, New Mexico, had been a growing community back in the '60s and '70s.

"By the looks of things, I think all of their big plans have gone out the window," Hank said to "Tiger"—the cat sunbathing in the doorway.

Lucky pulled in the drive and Hank waved him down. "Any luck?"

"Still looking," says Lucky as he got out of his wrecker. Lucky launched into a well-rehearsed litany of every junk yard, every parts supplier he had called within a 100-mile radius. "Cash for Clunkers. That's your problem."

"Huh?"

"It's against the law to part out all those cars traded in for government money. They all been crushed," Lucky said. "Bottom line is that it's not that easy. You got to understand, with them old vehicles, things like this don't happen overnight, especially with them Mopars. I'll look at the radiator and check out a couple of other things in the morning."

Lucky showed up in the morning, checked the radiator, repaired some wires and gauges, and did some other fiddling around under the hood. Hank wondered why Lucky was dressed in camouflage with a nine-inch blade hanging from his belt.

"Okay. See you in a couple of days. Just heard there's wild boar in the area."

"What does that have to do with anything?"

"Now that's some good eatin'. I'll bring ya back some."

"You've got to be kidding?"

Lucky shrugged his shoulders and drove off.

With the shop closed up tight for the night, Hank punched in Joe's number and hoped the call would go through this time.

"Hank, are you okay? I was just getting ready to drive out there! Did you get stuck in that mudslide?"

"Well, I wish I could say I was better. And, to answer your question, no, I was already way past Mojave when it happened. But, I am stuck. In some little one-horse town called Bella Vista. Which is everything but beautiful and it's certainly not a vista."

"What happened?"

"Threw a rod. Engine's fried."

"How?"

"Ask Potter."

"Oh, I'm sorry Hank. How can I help?"

"Do you know what tarantulas like to eat?"

"What?"

"I got a roommate. A tarantula. I named him Fred. Not big on conversation, but he's a good listener."

"Ha ha. Now that's a miracle. Ole Hank making this a laughing matter." Hank could hear the smile in Joe's voice. "But, where is Bella Vista, exactly?

"Somewhere east of Albuquerque."

"Albuquerque? You don't say. I know a guy there. It's been a few years, but let me give him a call."

"Okay. Thanks, Joe," Hank said as he ended the call. "Deadville is starting to get on my nerves!" Hank yelled into the dark.

The thought of staying one more night in the van was making Hank feel like Jack Nicholson in *The Shining.*

Out of sandwiches, Hank resolved to walk the four miles into town for something to eat. As he was walking down the road, a kid J.R.'s age pulled up in a nice-looking Tacoma.

"Hey mister. Need a ride?"

"Sure, kid. Can you take me somewhere to eat? I'm afraid I'm about to go mad if I have to wait at Lucky's another hour."

"Lucky's? How long have you been there?" He didn't give Hank time to answer. "Look, you can explain later. My name's Eddie. Let me just get you somewhere to eat."

"Thanks Eddie. I'll treat."

Eddie squeezed the Tacoma into a full lot of cars in front of a diner called "Maggie's Place". A hand-painted sign said the place was open from 7-7 six days a week and for dinner on Sundays. A short, middle-aged lady with bright red hair greeted them with open arms.

"Come on in, guys, and take a load off."

"Thanks Maggie. I brought a weary traveler with me," said Eddie. "Actually, he's been stuck at Lucky's."

"Oh, another one?" said Maggie. "Poor baby. That explains things. It's on the house, then. Find a table and make yourselves at home."

All of the tables were full, but an elderly couple motioned them over to their booth.

"We heard you're stuck over at Lucky's," the old man said.

"News sure travels fast around here," said Hank.

"Yep, even before it comes out of your mouth, someone already knows about it," laughed the old woman.

A young waiter with a stubbly beard took their orders. Eddie ordered a burrito. Hank thought he'd play it safe with a chicken-fried steak, mashed potatoes, green beans, and biscuits, and some coffee and apple pie.

Small talk aside, the elderly couple and Eddie agreed that Hank had better find someone other than Lucky to replace his engine.

"Unless you've got one of those old Chevys," the old man said.

"The Texaco across the street might be able to help," suggested Eddie.

"What about some of the men at the church, Ernie? A lot of 'em are into classic cars," the old woman said. "Why don't you come to church with us tomorrow and we'll introduce you?"

"Sure. Why not?" said Hank, smiling. But behind his smile, there was some angst. He hadn't been to church in ages and he really felt like sleeping in. But it *was* only one day and he might find someone who was willing to help him out.

The waiter brought out the meals, asked if they needed anything else before he said a little prayer over the food. Hank found it interesting that nobody in the restaurant even noticed.

"Why don't you stay at that little motel right next to Maggie's and we'll pick you up for church in the morning?" the old man offered.

"I can take you back to Lucky's to pick up your stuff," said Eddie.

"It's a done deal," said Hank in between mouthfuls.

The next morning, when they pulled into the church parking lot, Hank was amazed at how many cars there were. There was a brand new black Lexus, a Prius, a few dusty pickups, a station wagon, and a handful of classic cars. What really stood out, though, was the metallic blue '63 Corvette Sting Ray. There was also a cluster of bikes, a bunch of customized Harleys, a couple of Kawasakis, and a vintage Triumph. Hank hoped it wasn't some kind of Hell's Angels church.

The sanctuary was full and as they walked into the vestibule, Hank heard a familiar voice say, "Come on in. Take a load off." Turns out the little lady with the bright red hair was also the preacher.

As Maggie preached, Hank's heart was filled with the Good News. He later learned that Maggie had bought the foreclosed church several years back and revitalized this place of worship for locals and travelers alike. The little grey-haired ladies from the old days took up the first few pews. The back rows were for the motorcycle club, and in between sat most of the town of all ages and colors. And, there was always room for visitors. In a strange way, they all seemed to blend together. Right before service ended, Maggie ended with her usual, "Don't talk the talk, walk the walk" sermon.

After the service, everyone piled into the hall to share a potluck meal on what looked like long wooden picnic benches and tables. Eddie led Hank through the crowd to a table with guys from the car club, Cruisers for Christ. They looked like a ragged bunch, not like the guys back home.

"Heard you're stuck at Lucky's," a guy named Mike said.

"Yeah, guess I'm not so lucky after all," said Hank, surprised he was actually making a joke about it.

"Heard there's lot of those wild hogs running," one of the guys said. "You probably won't see Lucky for a couple of weeks."

"Eddie tells me that you and your wife were youth counselors," said Mike. "My wife Bonnie and I head the youth group here."

"Yes, we were. Long ago," said Hank, feeling a bit nostalgic. Hank perceived Mike's changing the subject to mean that no one had any solutions for getting Hank out of Bella Vista anytime soon. He would just have to be patient and wait for Lucky to return.

"We just had a classic car show here last weekend," said Bonnie. "Too bad you missed it. The kids could have benefited from hearing about your road trip."

"What a great idea," said Hank, perking up a bit. "I never thought of getting the kids interested in classic cars."

The next morning, when Hank learned that Lucky was still away, he extended his stay at the Bella Vista motel for a week.

No sense in rotting in that dust bowl.

When Hank got back to his room, Mike from the church called, inviting him to ride with the motorcycle club to the Route 66 museum in Tucumcari.

"Of course!" he exclaimed.

Classic cars, gas pumps, license plates. Real road history. Hank was surrounded by car nostalgia. *And to ride there with a bike club!*

To make small talk, Hank asked some of the guys if they had heard of the Lonely Ramblers.

"The band is going to be playing at Western's bar on the weekend. After that, it's rumored they're heading to Bella Vista."

Before he left, Hank asked someone to take a picture of him sitting on a Harley in front of the famous sand monument with a huge *66* on top. Then, he rode to Bella Vista on the back of that bike with a gruff-looking gal named Shirley. She didn't say much, and when they parted, she just waved with her gloved left fist, her right hand cranking back the throttle as her Harley sped away with that deep sound of Harley power.

The next day, Hank got a call from a Mr. Lujan who said he'd located the parts needed to fix the engine.

"Well, thank you," Hank said. "By the way, do I know you?"

"Joe says hi," Mr. Lujan responded.

"Oh, I see. Well, thank you. But, I still need an engine though."

"You should be getting a call about that as soon as we hang up," he said.

The phone rang again. It was Mike from the car club.

"Hey Hank. One of our members has an old engine that still works. It's just been sitting in his garage! There's just one thing."

"Uh-huh."

"Well, we need to see if Lucky will let us use his engine hoist. That shouldn't be a problem. It's just..."

"Yeah?"

"Well, Shirley, you know that gal you rode back from the museum with? She said she can get a hold of Lucky. Got his cell number. But..."

"Yeah?"

"She wants to meet you tomorrow night for a drink. Is that okay?"

Hank paused a moment.

One little drink couldn't hurt. What the heck?

"Sure. No problem." Hank was willing to do almost anything to get out of there.

"Great. I'll let her know. Once we have an okay from Lucky, you should be on the road by the end of the week."

"Mike, what do I owe you guys?"

"Nothing, Hank."

"What do you mean nothing?"

"Consider it a favor. Just pass it along, okay?"

Hank thought about the events of the past week. He had left California for good, averted a mudslide, took his picture in Winslow, Arizona, slept in a trailer park, tried a Christmas medley of hot peppers, got unlucky at Lucky's, befriended a tarantula, rode on the back of a Harley with a tough biker chick, and now he had been bribed to go out with her for a drink, and he agreed! Just a month ago, he would have been spending his days visiting the cemetery, eating the same breakfast at the diner, complaining for the sake of complaining, and maybe hanging out with Joe.

All Saints Day

Since he had first gotten marooned at Lucky's place, Hank had been dreaming of blowing out of town, kicking up some dust on that "You've got a friend in Bella Vista" sign, spitting out the window, and never looking back.

"Come on in and take a load off," Maggie said as she extended her arms and hugged Hank warmly. "How does it feel to have your van all fixed and ready to head east to go see that daughter and son-in-law now?"

"Feels great, Maggie. How are you today?"

"Very well. Fine. Thank you, Hank. We'll get you something to eat for the road. On the house!"

"I don't know how you stay in business, Maggie."

"God provides."

"That I can personally attest to," Hank said with a glow on his face.

Maggie nodded in Linda's direction with a smile. "Whatever Hank wants Miss Linda."

"Yes, ma'am," Linda said. "Well, hello Mr. Hank. Would you like some coffee?"

Hank nodded as he stopped at the counter to chat with the waitresses who usually had some small-town gossip to share. Faces scrubbed clean, they were all rosy-cheeked and cheery-eyed. Linda reminded him of Anne when she was in her twenties. A real beauty. Didn't need to wear any makeup.

"So, Linda, what do you recommend for my last meal in Bella Vista?"

They all gave him a funny glance. "The last time I heard someone say that, was when my momma said that Mr. Willard ate here and when he left..."

"Linda, don't..." Jonelle interrupted, placing her palm firmly on Linda's forearm. "Don't ever bring that up that again. That happened before you were even born."

"Momma says I was one-year-old."

"Ladies, I meant to say...I'm heading back east today. Van's all fixed up and ready to go."

"That's great news, Hank."

The waitresses went back to small talk, thankfully. Talking about things like Lucky still having not returned.

"Some say he got jabbed by a hog and was laid up in a hospital just over the border. Others say he got ten hogs and was butchering them and selling them to some restaurant owner next town over."

One of the girls talked about a vacation she was taking with her husband and kids to the Grand Canyon this summer. Another complained that her old man's idea of a vacation was visiting his mother in Oklahoma.

But, then came that inevitable question about Shirley.

"Well, how did it go?" Hank's face heated up as the waitresses were smiling at him waiting for an answer.

"Now, that's not a nice thing to ask. Maybe *that's* why he's leaving town in such a hurry," joked Linda. The girls laughed.

"Now girls, it wasn't a date," Hank weaseled, trying to dodge a four-on-one interrogation. "Really."

"Sure, Mr. Hank. We believe you," laughed Linda.

"Guess he's not going to kiss and tell?" Jonelle said leaving the question open to interpretation.

"I'm not telling you girls anything," laughed Hank as he headed toward his table. "Guess you'll just have to discuss it amongst yourselves and come up with your own stories."

"Wait, you didn't tell us about the Lonely Ramblers. Were they any good?"

Hank sat down and Linda poured him a cup of strong coffee with double cream. The cook brought a large plate of enchiladas with a fried egg on the side, and some sopapillos drizzled in honey.

"Looks delicious," Hank said.

He ate slowly, watching the doorway, hoping some of the town folks might stop by, but Maggie's place was unusually empty today. He left a generous tip and said his goodbyes to the waitresses, letting the door flap behind him. His heart was sore.

As he continued his drive down the main drag, he waved to a thin, dark-skinned man wearing a pair of faded Levis selling the last roasted green chiles of the season. Hank pulled over and bought a handful of green chile jerky, too. Just for the road. Heading toward I-40, he passed the Bella

Vista bar where he had had a margarita with Shirley the night before.

Behind all the leather and studs, she was a quiet gal. They spent most of the night talking about his road trip. She had been living on the road, too, but she ended up stopping in Bella Vista when she ran out of money, and she never left.

He thought about Maggie. Such a kind, giving person. The fellas in the off-road truck club were really good guys. Hank hadn't wasted his time in Bella Vista. No, Bella Vista was where he experienced real community.

Goodbye Lucky's Not-So-Super-Service Center! He made a sharp U-turn and drove into the dusty lot. No one was there except Tiger lazing on the hot metal chair out front.

With stealth, he parked his van behind the extra bay, rummaged through his tool box, and tiptoed to the front of the lot. He thought those damn rusty screws holding up the horseshoes on Lucky's sign might stop him from leaving his mark on this town, but he got them off, and put those horseshoes right back where they belonged: Upside down!

Serves Lucky right. Might even remind him to treat his future customers better.

Then, he checked back into the Bella Vista motel for the night.

"Why Mr. Hank. Please don't tell me you got van problems again," said Sue Mason, the owner.

"Actually, I've got a bad case of the Bella Vista blues."

She smiled and handed him the key to his old room. "Sounds like good words for a tune."

The place was a little ragtag, but Hank didn't care. He sat on the flowered bedspread and called Mike and Bonnie to see if they wanted to get together for lunch. Mike said they couldn't because they were busy this afternoon, taking the youth group on a trip.

"Hey, Hank," Mike added as a sort of spur-of-the-moment idea. "I know it's short notice, but why don't you come with us? We've got an extra seat or two. It's just a day trip and we'd all love to have you."

"Uh...sure. I mean absolutely!" Hank agreed to meet them in an hour.

He took out a stick of jerky and started chewing. He was part of the community here. Yes, even more so than with the guys back at the Happy Daze Geezer Club. Except for Joe. Which reminded him. He needed to call his old friend and tell him that the van had been fixed, and to thank him for having Lujan get the parts. Plus, he wanted to know how Judy was doing. He knew he had to call Kate, too.

He called Kate first, and it went straight to voicemail.

"Hi. This is Kate, Matt, and baby-to-be. Leave us a message and we'll get back to you. Have a great day!"

"Hi Kate. This is Dad. I wanted to tell you, well, surprise you but I wanted to let you know that...well, I'm heading back east to see you and Matt. And, I brought your mother with me. I mean her ashes with me so we can honor her last wishes."

That was it. Those were the words in his heart. He hadn't stated them as eloquently as he would have liked, but the deed was done. He hated leaving messages that people might not bother listening to. But, the silence on the other side of the line made it easier.

He headed to the church and parked in the lot. There were a few stragglers in the field talking, goofing off, and whistling. A couple of the bikers were riding in, and there was Bonnie chatting with the bus driver. A younger lady in a yellow cotton dress flagged Hank down.

"Hey, Hank." She walked a little closer.

"Shirley?"

"Have you already forgotten me?" Shirley smiled wryly.

"No, it's just. . ."

"You're used to seeing me in leather?"

"Yeah, something like that. You look...you look real pretty."

"Why, thank you, Hank. I always like to dress up when we go to Miss Myrtle's."

"Miss Myrtle's?"

"She's an old widow. No one knows how old she is. But, I'd guess she's seen about 100 years," Shirley said. "But she acts like she's only half that!"

"Hank, so glad you could come," said Bonnie giving him a hug. "Maybe you can tell the kids about your road trip while we ride on the bus."

About 15 kids, some of the off-road truck club guys and a few bikers, plus Mike, Bonnie, Shirley, and Hank all piled into a big old yellow school bus.

They pulled off of I-40 just before San Jon and headed back east on the old Route 66. Hank and Anne had planned on taking the scenic route, but Hank had forgotten that until now. They headed south on one of the Quay County roads that outlined the river. As they drove through miles of desert, Hank retold the story of his road trip to the school kids and got just up to the part where he was about to say some *choice words* about Ole Lucky.

"So, is it going to be a girl or a boy?" a young girl asked.

"What?"

"Your grandbaby, Grandpa Hank."

Just where road met the river, an old woman beating a rug in front of an old Victorian mansion appeared at a split in the road.

"It's Grandma Myrtle!" some of the kids cried.

The kids scrambled off of the bus and ran up to the frail-looking granny. One of the little girls wouldn't let go of her waist.

"Well, well, well. It's so good to see you all. How about some lemonade?"

Two young women in their twenties came from out back to greet them. One had two babies on each hip. An older girl went straight from the bus, took one of the babies, and swung her up and down until she was giggling uncontrollably. A shy little boy stood behind a line of laundry taking sneak peeks at the visitors.

"Miss Myrtle takes in single moms and their kids. We come to help them with cooking, cleaning, laundry, helping the kids to read. Anything that Miss Myrtle asks us to do," Shirley spoke quietly to fill him in on why they were there.

Hank was amazed. What a selfless way to spend a Saturday afternoon. The older kids all ran off in different directions and got to work stacking bales of hay, picking lettuce, and weeding the garden.

"Looks like a nice day to get this garage painted. What do you think?" Miss Myrtle asked Linda and Hank.

"Hank, this is Miss Myrtle. Miss Myrtle, Hank" Shirley made the introductions. "Hank's just passing through."

"So, what do you think of my granddaughter, Hank?"

"Hush now, Miss Myrtle. And, we're not dressed for painting."

"I always did tell you to wear your Sunday best. When you look good, you are good." Shirley smiled a bright and healthy grin. "What do you say, Hank? There's a couple of pairs of old overalls in that shed. Get yourself changed and grab a bucket of paint. You too, Shirley."

"Yes, Miss Myrtle."

They got the garage painted, cut the lawn, tended to the chickens, folded the laundry, read books to the little ones, cleaned up after dinner, and did other chores.

It was dark when they left on the bus. Hank sat next to Shirley who now had white "highlights" in her hair, thanks to Hank.

"I've never been so joyously exhausted in my life," Hank whispered to Shirley. When she didn't respond, Hank noticed that her head was bobbing. Quietly, he reached over with his right hand and gently rested her head against his shoulder.

The next morning, Hank was up before dawn and was one of the first ones to arrive at the church. This was the first time in his life that he actually wanted to hear a sermon. Maggie said it was All Saints Day, a day of remembrance of all the loved ones that have already gone to their rest. Hank was surprised that Maggie mentioned Anne, and he was glad that he had set her ashes next to him.

"God will never give you more than you can handle," Maggie began.

"Many of us on this All Saints Sunday have been or are in the midst of an overwhelming loss. And maybe you blamed God, as I blamed God for my own father's death. We keep thinking as we are trying to get through this, God won't give me more than I can handle and I am not handling it at all.

There must be something wrong with me or wrong with God."

Hank felt a rumbling in his pocket. *Who in the heck was calling him on a Sunday morning? Maybe it was Joe? He was never an early riser.*

"So...if you've just lost a parent, a spouse, a sibling, or a child, or a friend or if your child has told you to get lost. If your job is being phased out or if your health is failing fast, you may feel that you've come to the end of your rope. You may think that all you can do is tie a knot and hang on."

"Don't do that. Just let go of trying to handle it yourself and let God. And as we do that, we will meet God in our mess. You'll find God managing the mess. It is now time to put it all in God's hands."

"Amen," many in the congregation said aloud.

"So when I hear people complain that they didn't meet God while worshipping, sometimes I wonder. God was here for you, but maybe you just weren't there for Him."

"Amen," said Hank. "Amen."

Maggie's words comforted Hank. He felt confident that no matter where his spiritual journey would lead him, even with all the detours, speed bumps, and repairs, he would be okay. He wouldn't worry anymore about his trip. He wouldn't worry about Kate. He was ready to let go of the past, accept what happened to Anne, realizing that it was God's plan after all.

"Remember my good people, don't just talk the talk, walk the walk."

"Amen!"

The church meal passed too quickly for Hank. He had wanted to spend the rest of the day breaking bread with his friends, but goodbye hugs would have to do. The most important thing was that he had accepted Jesus as his Saviour. Now, he recognized that he wouldn't be walking his journey alone.

As he was leaving, he spotted Shirley in the crowd and reached out for her hand. "You should have told me, Shirley."

"Would it have made a difference?"

"It would have helped me understand you better."

"I didn't want you to think less of me, Hank."

"Less of you? Why, honey, it makes me feel more compassion for you. Having to grow up without parents. Bless Miss Myrtle for taking you in."

"Amen to that, Hank. She is a Godly woman. Hank, just be safe. And Hank?"

"Yeah?"

"Thanks for letting me get to know you a little bit."

"You have my number. You know I hate texting. But, if it's from you, I'll text you back."

He gave her a long, firm hug, put her hand in his and squeezed it.

As he set out on his way, he knew he should forgive Lucky. In fact, if Lucky hadn't been so irresponsible, Hank would never have met the good folks of Bella Vista.

I guess the Sherriff's Deputy was right, 'Lucky is good people,' Hank grinned, adding aloud, "in a Lucky kind of way."

America Whizzes by at 65 MPH

Rejuvenated by the church service and the fellowship, Hank felt ready to get on the road again. He didn't get to visit the Grand Canyon or the Hoover Dam, but he did get to drive on Route 66 with a bunch of school kids on a mission trip to help out an old widow, who in turn, helps out "widows" and orphans.

"Don't mess with Texas," he said as he passed the Texas State Line. That phrase was smothered over every souvenir shot glass at one of those travel lodges where he had stopped with his young family so many years ago. Today, he certainly wouldn't be messing with Texas because he needed to make up weeks' worth of travel in two days, especially if he wanted to avoid snow. No time for coffee. No time for bathroom breaks either. All he had to do was drive the long, great road before him amidst blue Texas skies and cowboys hauling gear in Texas edition Silverados. Hank clung to the far right lane to avoid the semis and four-wheel-drive trucks that were racing to Oklahoma. They sure drive faster in Texas, too, he thought.

A text came in. It was from Shirley. "I miss you already," it said.

No texting while driving. Eyes on the road. We're on a mission.

Hank suspected that the Mr. Willard the girls at the restaurant were talking about was somehow a part of Shirley's story. If Linda was no more than 25 years old, Mr. Willard must have had his "last meal" about 24 years ago. Shirley looked about 40, so that would put her at about 16 years old when it happened, probably around the age she was when Miss Myrtle took her in. The mystery might be solved if he asked Shirley her last name.

You don't ask ladies who think you should know their last name what their last name is, Hank. Bad idea, Hank. Bad idea.

And, if Shirley *were* 40 years old, she was a bit too young for Hank. Maybe she looked younger than she really was?

Maybe, if she were 45...I might consider it.

But, what was he considering? What was *it*? He couldn't get involved with someone who was getting farther and farther away by the minute. He had too much road to cover, and he had to put Anne to rest before he could even begin thinking about *it*, whatever *it* was. Well, not exactly, because he was already thinking about *it*.

The church service was enlightening. The fellowship, warming to the soul. But, holding Shirley's hand? There was no word for what he felt at that moment. Since Anne's passing, he had forgotten what it felt like to really connect with someone. He hoped the miles increasing between them minute by minute would make this "missing" feeling go away.

Amarillo! Hank hadn't seen traffic like this in weeks. Next, he whizzed through the small Texas towns of Groom, McLean, and Shamrock, and wondered if that might be a lucky place to stop. Yahoo! Oklahoma State Line. Exit 1. Texola. A near ghost town just beyond the border. Ride baby ride! His stomach growled as he passed one of those gigantic travel stops with semi after semi lined up. He passed a few more stops, wishing that the uncomfortable rumbling in his stomach would go away. When it didn't, he stopped off in a town that should have been called "Dirt Poor City."

Mawmaw's Gas. Now, that sounded like a friendly place. It had the old style type pumps that didn't even take a credit card. He flipped down the handle and the gas came out. As he was filling her up, he watched the number wheels turn and click, then he walked into the station to pay.

"How much gas ya get?" asked a young man sitting behind the counter with a cowboy hat slanted over his eyes.

"You can't tell?" Hank asked.

"Naw. Our pumps ain't workin' right. We jus' ask people when they come in."

Hank stumbled a bit. "Uh, about 20 gallons."

"Are you hungry? Mawmaw makes great sandwiches." He pointed to a cooler. "If you need a place to stay, we're renting our extra room for just $15 a night."

"Maybe I'll have a sandwich," Hank said. The cooler was empty.

"I'll ask her to make you one right away. A fresh one."

Everything about the place was clean. There was not a spec of dirt in it, which was amazing since the town was one big dirt heap.

"Why not?" Hank said feeling adventurous.

Hank reread Shirley's message and wondered if he should text her back. He had promised her he would if she did, but now he was hesitant.

First of all, this texting thing was complicated. Hank tried to convince himself, even though he had been texting Joe and Kate throughout his trip.

Secondly, he didn't want to give Shirley the wrong impression.

"Here you go, Mister. Mawmaw's triple special. Turkey, ham, real roast beef. Two kinds of cheeses. Lettuce, tomato, and Mom's special sauce."

"That was fast," said Hank. "How much?" Hank wondered what the kid meant by *real* roast beef.

"$37.60 for the gas. The sandwich makes it an even $40. And, I'll throw in washin' your windows for free. Don't want no accidents, ya know."

"Great idea. Thanks." Hank had gotten used to looking through the dust and the bugs since he left Bella Vista.

"Can I fill you up with some washer fluid, too?"

"No, thanks. It...it doesn't work anyway."

"Why don't you let me have a look at it," the kid said.

It was already 1:37, and Hank wanted to make it to the Tri-State border before nightfall. Still, the kid had a point.

The kid looked under the dash and rummaged around a bit. He was so thin Hank thought he might get lost in his cowboy hat. He dusted his hands on his pants, ran back to the shop, and brought back an old tin can. Hank was hoping that the kid wasn't a Potter or Lucky Jr. The kid went back to work for a few minutes then turned around and said, "I jimmied it up. Should hold you at least until Oklahoma City."

"Thanks," Hank said as he reached out his hand. The cowboy stuck out his hand and shook hard but was surprised when he felt the folded up $10 bill.

"Thank you, sir. Be careful out there an' come on back now."

Hank got back on I-40 with clean windshields, a full tank of gas, and a pretty decent sandwich. He just had to hit the window washer button, and it worked! As he neared Oklahoma City, traffic picked up, but Hank didn't feel like stopping. He was making good time and was itching to get to the I-44 interchange in Tulsa. He kept up with the traffic all the way to Vinita, where he stopped off at what was once the world's largest McDonalds, spanning the interstate below. Hank ordered a coffee and a burger and figured he ought to listen to Joe's voicemail.

"Uh, hi Dad. This is Kate. I got your message....we... out o tow and ... surprise... small house...don't know...Really? Call...back."

Hank listened to it again. The message was clear. Kate didn't want him there.

His phone rang.

"Hank here."

"Well, that's a friendly greeting. How's it going?"

"If you would have called about five minutes ago, I would have said just peachy."

"Are you broke down again?"

"I might as well be. Kate just doesn't want me to come out there."

"That's the most ridiculous thing I've ever heard, Hank."

"Do you want me to replay the message so you can hear it for yourself?"

"Can that dinosaur of a phone of yours do that?"

"Whatever."

"Look, Hank. Whatever Kate says, you're a man on a mission. You promised Anne. After that, you're a free man. Still, it's hard for me to believe that Kate wouldn't want you there. Check the voicemail again and call me later."

"Hey Joe?"

"What?"

"I need you to do me a favor. Can you do one of those internet searches...on a guy by the last name of Willard? From Bella Vista, New Mexico ...like 24 or 25 years ago?"

As Hank watched the sky darken from the massive golden arches that graced the highway below, he recalled just how breathtaking the desert sunset had been on his last night in Bella Vista. Crisp red and subdued layers of yellow strata blanketing the autumn desert sands and dunes. Sharing the view with Shirley at Miss Myrtle's made it even more special. Hank lumbered back to the van and got back onto the highway, knowing he had made the right decision. No matter what Kate had said in her voicemail message, he needed to say his final goodbye to Anne. He turned on the radio, fumbled with the old tuning knob, and stopped on a classic rock station. Then their song came on. His and Anne's. He abruptly turned it off. He was not in any mood for nostalgia.

As each mile clipped by, he daydreamed about his reunion with Kate. He would show up at her doorstop and apologize for missing her teenage years. She would slam the door in his face. Matt would pry the door open and make her tell him she was sorry. And, then, he would apologize to a sliver of light coming through the doorway and be on his way. A lone, huge raindrop plopped onto the windshield bringing him out of his daydream. Then another and another. He listened to the slapping of the old wipers for the next several hours until the light blue evening sky broke through. "Dutchman's Pants" his grandmother used to call them.

Just as the sky cleared, he passed a large sign that read, "Jesus is Lord – Not a Swear Word. One mile."

"So true," said Hank aloud. "So true. Might be a good place to stop for the night." He pulled off of the interstate and saw that the place looked like an ordinary truck stop, except for a sign on an old semi-trailer that read *Transport for Christ*. Hank made a mental note to visit if he ever stopped by this way again on a Sunday. And, with Kate acting the way she was, that might happen much sooner than he thought. But, he couldn't go back to Bakersfield. He had closed that door. What about Bella Vista? He just didn't know. He walked past a bunch of good ole boys, cussing, smoking, drinking, and just hanging out. They had hit their limit behind the wheel of the big rigs and had nothing better to do for the rest of the day. He wondered if this truck stop had ever changed anyone's life. He sure hoped it did for these guys, just like Bella Vista did for him.

"Damn, I used to have one just like it," one of the guys said. "That's a real nice van."

"Thanks. Hey, you guys know of a good place to bunk down for the night?"

"You're looking at it," one of the truckers says. "Wanna join us?"

"Here, wanna pop a top, Pops?" laughed one of the guys. "Just got it out of the cooler."

Hank hadn't ever hung out with truckers, but he was too tired to keep driving and something in his heart told him these guys were a good bunch. "Sure. I'm done for the night. I'd love a beer to wash that west Texas dust off my wind pipe."

A few of the guys shared their latest tales on the road. A guy named Hal was listening to what he called "a good book on tape" called *The Notebook*. Hank eventually felt relaxed enough to tell the guys about his adventures in Bella Vista.

"Lucky's the reason none of us ever stop there anymore. Now you know why," laughed one of the guys.

"You know Lucky?"

"Yeah, most of us do."

"Cheap son of a gun."

"Well, since you know Lucky, do you guys know anything about a guy named Willard?" asked Hank.

"Damn shame," said one of the old school guys. "That was a long time ago. Some things are better off left unsaid. You know what I mean?"

"Who's Willard?" asked one of the younger truckers.

"That was before your time kid. Leave it be."

Hank wanted to pry, but he didn't. He thanked them for the beer and lumbered back to his van, turned on the ignition, making sure to park it away from the blaring lights of the truck stop and far enough away from the rigs. He was going to sleep through the night if he could.

The next morning was an unusually warm, bright sunny November day. Two more days and he would be taking Anne home to the banks of the beautiful Chesapeake Bay, with or without Kate. He got up at 7 a.m., ordered a coffee and donut from the truck stop, and saw that the chapel door was ajar. He decided to take a look inside. It was simple. A few rows of chairs, an altar, and a large, wooden hanging crucifix.

"Anybody here?" Hank asked.

He could hear someone milling around in the back. "Hello, anybody here?"

"We're not open now," a stern voice said. "Come back on Sunday."

"My name's Hank," Hank said.

"Are you the one who is supposed to pay me?" she asked.

"No, Ma'am. I'm just passing through."

"My granddaughter is sick and I need to buy her medicine today. I've been cleaning this place for days, getting it ready for their Sunday service, and…"

"Well, can I help you?" Hank offered.

"Here, grab a rag," she said.

The old woman explained how her daughter could no longer take care of her granddaughter, but she didn't say why. She loved her granddaughter, but felt resentful about being forced into the role of parent again. She had to work two extra jobs and care for a five-year-old. The burden was great.

Hank just listened and cleaned. The woman seemed to feel better after she was able to talk to someone. He gave her a $20 bill to help pay for her granddaughter's medicine, and left a $10 donation for the church.

"Would you come back here on Sunday and light a candle for your granddaughter for me?" Hank asked the old woman. "I'm just passing through. Otherwise, I would." She kept cleaning with a determined look on her face, but she nodded that she would.

8:15 am. Hank was back on the road. Miles sped by, city by city, county by county. The old van was still running perfect. The car club guys back in Bella Vista were right. Nothing was wrong with the new motor. The owner of the Duster just had a need for speed, and that is how Hank ended up with the old slant six "Leaning Tower of Power". The van wasn't going to burn rubber, but it sure kept up with the traffic.

America's landscape continued to whiz by at 65 miles an hour. Occasionally, car horns blew as Hank drove by, giving the old girl a thumbs up. Dan was going to love this van. Especially since it had been practically rebuilt: New tires, shocks, exhaust, brakes, radiator, and now a rebuilt engine. Just like Hank, the van was on its way to having a restored heart and soul.

Once the kid repaints it and does the interior, all it might need is a transmission, and she will be just like new.

As he neared St. Louis, Hank, hands glued to the wheel, was suddenly plagued with too many highway choices. Should he take I-64 or I-55? What about the bypass? Before he could decide, he ended up on I-55 heading north. Now what? He couldn't turn around because he didn't know where he would end up. And, with the congested traffic driving at a fast pace, he started to feel nauseous. There were so many exits and so many cars. The arch and the downtown area and the Mississippi became a blur. All he wanted to see was the sign for I-70.

Finally. There it is. Thank you, Lord!

Heading east again, he passed through Brownstown, St. Elmo, Effington, Woodsbury, Jewett, Casey. He wanted to make it to the Indiana State Line, but that wasn't going to happen. He saw a sign for a campground, pulled over and slept another night in his "camper" van. He paid $12 for the spot, woke up before any talkative campers could delay him, and got back on the road.

Onward he drove through Terra Haute and Indianapolis, and all of the little towns in between. Occasionally, his mind drifted back to the little desert town of Bella Vista. It was a simple town, and a quiet town, but far from boring. His legs and back began to ache, so today was going to be a short driving day. If he could make it to the east side of Columbus, he would avoid tomorrow's morning traffic. Yep, tonight he was going to splurge on a motel room. His old body just couldn't take another night of sleeping in the van.

As he exited the interstate and drove down the main drag of a little town called Buckeye Hills, classic car after classic car passed him on the road. The front desk clerk at the inn told him they had had a wet fall this year and that the monthly car cruises had been rained out twice. So, with the unusually warm weather, the town was holding an impromptu late season cruise. Today and through the weekend.

"The town usually shuts down, and most businesses close early except for the restaurants and hotels," the clerk said. "You got our last room."

"That's great news. Do you think I can enter my van?"

The clerk peeked outside the window. "Under all that dirt? Drive her around out back by our shuttlebus and we'll hose her down," the clerk said. "That's a pretty cool-looking van though."

"I've gotten more attention driving her than if I had a Mustang or a Camaro," Hank said. "Maybe I should have kept the old gal, but she's promised to another."

"That's what girls will do to you," the clerk laughed.

Once Hank got to Main Street, classic cars lined both sides of the street. American flags were waving at every light post, and in the center of town there was a gazebo where the high school brass band was playing. A barbershop quartet dressed in red and white striped shirts and bowties was waiting to perform. Old style clapboard houses with ruffled American flags draped over their front porch railings and decorated with the last of the fall potted flowers made the place look like something out of yesteryear.

"I haven't had to parallel park in years," Hank said under his breath as he barely pulled the van into place. "Especially, not a van."

"I haven't seen one of these in years that has looked so well-preserved," said a thin gentleman with a handlebar moustache as he rubbed his hand over the hood of the old van. "How did you keep her from rusting?"

"She's been stowed away in sunny southern California," Hank laughed.

Hank spent the next few hours talking to folks about his journey from California to Maryland and everything in between.

"What a great idea. We should take the kids on a coast-to-coast road trip over the summer and stop in small towns along the way, honey," a young mother with two little kids said to her husband.

The crowd started to thin as folks went to get some supper at the diner. It was now Hank's turn to walk down Main Street to have a look at the cars. He ran into one of the locals.

"You're still driving the first car you've ever owned? Amazing!" Hank exclaimed.

Jon told Hank his muscle car story. It all started in the late '60s. Jon was just a regular teenager who had fallen in love with Muscle cars right before the craze hit. Then he got drafted.

"Before I went to Nam, I was just a kid—a kid who memorized every word in every car magazine ever published. Then, when I knew I was going in, I started planning on what I was gonna buy with all that cash I'd save up during my tour of duty."

"Eighteen months later, when I got out, my mom and dad picked me up at that Greyhound station. You probably drove right by it, just a mile up the road. They looked different. Mom's hair had turned completely white and Dad, well, he was rail thin."

"We drove right by S&S's Pontiac—long gone now—and there she was, that '71 Blue Trans Am with a 455 motor. I asked my folks to stop then and there and I bought her straight outta the showroom. Man, did I have a stack of tickets from drag racing. Don't know if I ever paid any of them."

Hank laughed and nodded in agreement.

"She helped me out, got me through everything, so I just wasn't gonna let her go," he sighed. "Working on her was better than talking to a shrink."

"I don't see how you could."

"Almost every day, somebody would offer me a wad of cash, but I'd never sell her."

Jon told Hank about how he drove his new wife, Sally, to their honeymoon in the Poconos in that car, and how he brought Sally and all three kids home from the hospital when they were born. "Yep, all three of the kids learned to drive in her."

Hank thanked Jon for the story and made his way to the diner. Parked right out front was a Plymouth Valiant, just like his first car. It had only cost him a couple hundred bucks, but it was worth a million when it came to his social life. It wasn't a hit at the A&P grocery parking lot where all the young people hung out, but because of it, he was definitely part of the gang, spending hours cruising around town, swapping stories, some true, and some fiction. Jon was right. There was more to a car than metal and parts. It was the people who drove them and the stories that happened in them that made them classics.

After a supper of mashed potatoes and pork roast and green beans and a baking powder biscuit with butter, Hank revved up the old van, feeling like he was part of something bigger than himself, kind of like a part of history. Maybe glorifying a little nostalgia was okay, he thought, just as long as he didn't get stuck in the past.

Slip Sliding Away

That night in Buckeye Hills, Hank slept in what he thought was the most comfortable bed in in the world—anything was more comfortable than sleeping in the van—and, with a belly full of good home cooking, and a spectacular evening at an unexpected car cruise, he felt as if he had just been fitted with a turbo boost.

He hopped out of bed, showered and shaved. Today was the last day. Yes, today, he would finally be bringing Anne home. This was the home stretch, the final leg of the marathon. Yesterday afternoon he had hit the wall, but today, he was as rejuvenated as ever. Another six or seven hours of driving? That was nothing compared to what he had been through over the last few weeks.

As he left the motel, it was evident that the mid-western Indian summer had ended. The last of the oranges, yellows, and reds that clung to the maples and oaks amidst that clear, blue Ohio sky, made it appear warmer than it really was. But, a little cold air wasn't going to stop him. In fact, it felt invigorating. He jumped into his refrigerator of a van and watched the steam of his warm breath condense on the windshield. He feathered the gas and turned the ignition. The van seemed to say, "Hey, I'm still sleeping," but after a few futile complaints, she gave in and started up.

He hopped onto I-70, the road that would lead him to Baltimore, via a few detours here and there in Maryland. First thing, he would stop off at the Little Tavern and get a burger and coffee, and gas up at one of his favorite high school hangouts, the red-roofed Exxon on Liberty Heights Boulevard. He remembered how he bugged old man Pollard to hire him as a pump attendant and window washer the summer before his senior year, and how folks used to get trading stamps based on how many gallons of gas they bought.

Hank's reminiscences were cut short, though, by a row of ugly, orange construction cones lined up mile after mile. It was slow-going, and for the duration of the traffic back-up, his only view was the unsightly back end of an SUV that badly needed washing. Stop and start and roll. Stop and start and roll. The flow of traffic finally picked up, but as he neared Wheeling, he came to a dead stop. Hank rolled down the window and popped his head out to see what the hold-up was. Was it an accident? More construction? As the highway curved, all he could see were dozens of cars and trucks lined up as if they were waiting to get out of a rock concert. The temperature had dropped at least ten degrees since he had left the motel, and the skies were starting to cloud up. "Sure glad I got those new tires in Bakersfield," laughed Hank, trying to remain positive. "Too bad they aren't snow tires, though."

His phone rumbled in his shirt pocket, and his stomach clenched at the thought that it might be Kate.

"Hey Hank, how's it going?"

"Oh, hi Joe."

"Were you expecting someone else?"

"Uh no. I'm just driving. I mean, I'm stuck here in traffic."

"You wanna hang up?"

"No, I'm pretty much stopped."

"Hear anything from Kate?"

"Not yet. I'm waiting for her to call back."

"Hmm, that sounds like a plan."

"What?"

"Does she even know you're coming?"

"Of course, she does."

"Well, I searched Google..."

"You what?"

"Didn't you ask me to look up something about your girlfriend?"

"You mean Shirley? No, she's just a good friend. That's all."

"Nothing wrong with that, Hank. We need all the friends we can get. How's the van holding up?"

"Slow to warm. Hey, Joe, about that search..."

"Why did you want me to check out some guy named Willard?"

"What did you find out?"

"Well...I don't think I should be telling you about it while you're driving."

Well, that was great. Joe didn't want to tell Hank about Willard either. How bad could it be?

"I'm gonna let you go, Hank. Keep it between the ditches pal."

The flow of traffic picked up. Hank had to see what all the fuss was about, but all he saw was a police cruiser and a tow truck flashing its lights on the berm. Looked like the end of a bad accident. Nothing had been blocking the road. Just gawkers slowing to take a look.

Hank revved the van to 65 mph. It felt good. Once he was clear of the police, he'd see if the old van could do 70. He'd just keep with the traffic flow. That's all. The Pennsylvania border was within reach, and after that, it would only be a two-hour drive to Maryland. The highway snaked through Pennsylvania, running through a city called Washington. Now, this was his section of the country. He got onto Highway 43, passing through a little town called California, drove over the Monongahela River to Uniontown where he connected to 119 then 40. Once he passed Elk Park and Addison, he would almost be back to his home state.

Finally. The Maryland State Line. He got onto I-68 and headed toward Grantsville. It felt freeing, like he could sprint all the way to Baltimore. He had almost forgotten how beautiful the Appalachians were.

As the highway climbed, large, wet flakes started to splatter onto the windshield. It was electrifying. He hadn't seen snow in years. Except for in the mountains in California. He turned on the radio to check out the forecast.

"...first snow of the season. Expect two to three inches to accumulate into the early evening. Temperatures expected in the high twenties tonight, folks. Slow down and drive safely out there," said a male voice on the radio with a sense of excitement.

The sky grew darker and Hank began to worry. Two to three inches of the white stuff wasn't a big deal for Marylanders, but snow and below-freezing temperatures would be a nightmare for him. As he continued to climb into the mountains, he got stuck behind a lumbering semi that splattered Hank's windshield with a mixture of slush, dirt, and gravel. He turned on the wipers, hoping that the Oklahoma cowboy's trick would still work.

"Damn. No more washer fluid. I should have listened to that kid and refilled in Oklahoma City."

For the next ten miles, salt sprayed from passing semis and trucks. The snowflakes came more quickly now, collecting on Hank's windshield. The van felt like it was sliding on black ice, so he slowed it down to 40 mph. His plan was to stick to the far right lane even if every car on the highway had to pass him. Between the window fogging up and the mud-snow mixture splattering his windshield, he could barely see the winding road before him. The van slid into the left lane. Hank instinctively jerked the wheel, and skidded onto the shoulder, narrowly missing an SUV.

Out of breath, Hank took a minute to gain his composure.

Felt like I did a 360. At least the van is facing the right way. Dammit. I didn't have to deal with this crap back in California. What the heck was I thinking?

He put the shifter into drive, eased on the gas pedal, and the van groaned. "Must be some snow on the shoulder," he muttered. He tried the gas again. Nothing.

Maybe I should pull out that shovel and dig myself out of this mess.

Traffic sped by as he wobbled out of the driver's side. Blinded by the shimmering headlights and biting flecks of snow, Hank sure wished he hadn't given away his favorite corduroy jacket. He crouched onto the wet pavement, but didn't see any snow or ice. Just black top.

Dodging the traffic, he jumped back into the van to give it another try. He put it into gear. It shuddered but it started.

It's the damn transmission. Dammit. And, I've got at least ten more miles 'til I reach Cumberland.

It took him more than one-half of an hour to reach the first Cumberland exit. There, a man-made oasis of sparking lights and 30 gas pumps with a large grocery and a car wash greeted him.

Hank felt let down. He knew what a faulty transmission meant. It meant a detour on the home stretch of his journey. It meant more money in repairs. It meant more hotel and restaurant bills.

The clerk in the grocery couldn't recommend a mechanic, but Hank kept his promise to God that he wouldn't sweat the small things, that he would put everything in God's hands. He pulled out of the station and decided to drive away from the highway, not really knowing where to go. The road was dark except for a few lone streetlights planted every quarter-mile or so. He stopped at a stop sign and watched how the snow rained down by the light of a dim streetlight. Beneath it was one of those '50s gas stations with no pumps, but with several cars parked under a retro-looking canopy. "Honest Charlie's Transmissions. We Get You Back into Gear" the sign on the outside read.

A light was still on in the shop. Hank drove through the tire tracks and parked the van. He dusted off his sneakers on the mat before opening the doors. A chime rang. Honest Charlie shouted from the bay that he was busy and to take a seat.

Hank noticed that above the doorway to the shop there was a placard that said, "As for me and my house, we will serve the LORD." Hank grabbed an old car magazine, but with tired eyes he just looked at the pictures. When Honest Charlie came out, Hank noticed that his shirt nametag said James.

"Let me lock up and we'll take her for a spin," he said.

During the drive, Hank found out that James took over Charlie's shop last year. He was Charlie's apprentice, and when Charlie was ready to retire, it seemed natural that he should hand over the shop to James. James had become like a son to Charlie. He had a good work ethic and faith in God. What more could he want for his shop that had served the locals for thirty years? Just after he retired, Charlie was laid to rest. Now the locals, out of deference to Charlie, called James "Old Charlie", and James didn't seem to mind at all. "Old Charlie" admitted, though, that he had a hard time running the place like a business while trying to help out his customers.

Hank felt like he had seen a ghost.

"Mr. Hank, what's wrong? You don't mind if I call you that?"

"No, Old Charlie. Mr. Hank is just fine. It's just that...that early on in my road trip, another fella named 'Old Charlie' also helped me out. It just sent some shivers down my spine. That's all."

"Well, looks like you're going to need major transmission work. Likely because this van's been sitting all these years. Very fortunate you didn't break down in the desert somewhere."

"Well, I did have it checked out in Bakersfield before I left. Guess that 'ole Potter didn't know what he was talking about." Hank wanted to call

Joe right then and there, and get Potter's number so he could give him a verbal beat down.

"Don't think I'll be able to get a rebuild kit real quick. Probably will take a week to get parts and fit it into the schedule. I know a great place where you can stay. It's called Terri's Cumberland Bed & Breakfast. All home cooking. You won't want to leave."

Hank didn't like the sound of that. It reminded him of his stint in Bella Vista. Not that it hadn't been great, but he was so close to getting home.

Hank left the keys with Old Charlie, called a cab, and entered the bed and breakfast. A dark-haired young lady with a warm smile called out, "Welcome home, honey. You look like you need a hot bath and an electric blanket."

"A nice hot pizza would go over well, too. Pepperoni," said Hank.

Terri asked Hank for his I.D. and ran his credit card. "I'll phone in an order for you. Here's the key. You're in Room 5. Down that hallway and to the right. Breakfast is from 6 to 8:30 a.m."

As soon as he got to his room, Hank turned up the heat to 80 degrees, got into bed and pulled the covers up to his neck. All he wanted was to fall asleep, but he had a pizza on the way, and he needed to call Kate and tell her he had been delayed. Again. He knew he should call, but he was so disappointed that he just sent a text.

Hi Kate. Dad. Sorry. I'm delayed. Van repairs. Can I stay at your place? Next week. Love, Dad

The phone rang.

"Well, that was fast," Hank said aloud. It was Old Charlie.

"Hi Hank. Seems like my buddy Carl found you a transmission kit. I think I can fit you into the schedule in the next three days. How does that sound?"

"What's the damage," sighed Hank.

"It's a modern unit with an extra gear. A lifetime service warranty. Probably improve your mileage too. I'll give it to you at 20% over my cost. You'll just need to pay for my labor."

"So the damage is...?"

"No more than $2,500."

Not good news for Dan, the van's new owner. Who would have thought that the stupid van was going to cost more than the sale price to get it going? You've got to either have deep pockets or a good, honest friend to work on these old Dodge vans.

"Sure, Old Charlie. Sounds like a deal. Thank you."

The phone rang again. It was a 443 area code. Kate!

"Dad. Are you okay? I've been trying to call you all day."

"Oh hi, Matt. You have? I'm fine. Just sitting in a hotel waiting for the van to get repaired."

"Where are you? I'll come and get you right away."

"Cumberland. But, don't come. I mean, the weather's bad. Anyway, we'd have to drive back to get the van once it's repaired."

"Dad!"

"I'm okay. Are you guys okay? Did you and Kate get my message? Are you both okay with the arrangement?"

"Dad, what do you mean? We're excited to see you. Keep me posted if you need anything. Call me tomorrow and let us know how you're doing, okay? Talk to you tomorrow."

"Okay. We'll talk tomorrow."

Well, that seemed promising. Still Hank was not sure why Matt called instead of Kate. Was she okay? Was she angry with him? He figured he would find out when he got to Baltimore. That is, if he got to Baltimore.

The phone rang. Was it Kate? No, it was the pizza delivery guy telling him his pizza was on the way. Another call was coming in and he tried to grab it but it went to voicemail.

He hit the redial button and James answered. "Yep?"

"Hey, this is Hank."

"Oh hey, Mr. Hank. I got some good news for you. Seems like I got a cancellation. I can start on your van tomorrow afternoon. How does that sound?"

"Sounding better and better every time you call, Old Charlie!"

"There's a catch, though. I'm busy tomorrow morning. So, I need you to pick up the transmission kit."

"Well, that might be a problem."

"I can stop by tomorrow morning at 7:30. You can take my truck. You drop me off at the shop, and I'll give you the keys. Shouldn't take you more than a half hour."

"Sounds good. Thanks, buddy."

Hank came down for breakfast the next morning at 6:30 a.m. The smell of sizzling bacon, eggs, and pancakes filled the air. Two local news anchors, an attractive man and lady, were talking on the T.V. about the weather. They looked like they never had driven a day in the snow! They said it was going to be a little warmer today. Hank felt relieved. The idea of having to drive Old Charlie's truck in the snow terrified him.

An older couple sitting at a table next to him asked Hank what brought him to Cumberland.

"Van repairs," he said stoically. "I've been on a cross-country road trip with this old Dodge van and this isn't the first time I've done this rodeo.

So, please don't mistake any frustration on my part for being rude."

"We're out here visiting our kids. They've got a small place and we needed some space," the lady said.

Hank shared a brief summary of the repairs in Bakersfield, the quick fix at the Little Hurtin' campgrounds, his three-week stay in Bella Vista, the young cowboy in Oklahoma, and his unexpected stay in Cumberland.

Terri brought out their breakfasts and the most delicious-looking scrapple that Hank had ever seen.

"Well, thank you, Terri. This looks great."

"It should keep you warmed up for most of the day," she said. "I know of an excellent restaurant where you can eat tonight."

"Thanks, Terri." Hank finished up the breakfast just as Old Charlie walked in. They got into his truck and Hank dropped the mechanic off at his shop.

"Mr. Hank, when I was putting your van into the bay last night, I noticed a heavy blue box sitting on the passenger side. It looked valuable, so I put it in our safe."

"You did?"

"Yeah, I did. I hope that's okay."

"Of course it is, Old Charlie. Thank you. Thank you." For the first time during the course of this trip, Hank had forgotten about Anne. He hoped she'd forgive him. He was grateful that Old Charlie had put her in a safe place.

"After I drop off the part, Old Charlie, I'd like to get the box out of the safe and head back to the B&B," Hank said.

"No problem, Hank. I can pick you up at 5 if you'd like to go to dinner with Terri and me."

That evening, Hank, Terri, and Old Charlie drove in Old Charlie's truck to a place called Nate's Family Restaurant. From the outside, it looked like it was closed. But, when they parked in the back, Hank could see that it was quite crowded. They ordered at the counter and seated themselves. Hank got a chicken-fried steak and mashed potatoes.

As they sat down, Hank looked at Old Charlie with a serious expression.

"I can't thank you enough for taking care of Anne today, Old Charlie."

"Anne?"

"That box you put in the safe? Those are my dear Anne's ashes. I'm bringing her home to Baltimore to her final resting place."

"Oh, I didn't know. Maybe, I should have called you first."

"No, it's okay. It's just…"

"Hank, I couldn't help but overhear your story in the breakfast room this morning," interrupted Terri. "Not that I was eavesdropping or anything."

"Oh, it's not much of a secret, Terri. So, Old Charlie, how's the van coming along?"

"Well, I've got some good news and some bad news. Which would you like first?"

"How about the good news?"

"After Terri filled me in on your story, I called Carl and got a break on the part, so everything should cost you around $1,500. I also bumped you up on the schedule. We should be done by tomorrow afternoon. How does that sound?"

"That's great news. Now, what's the bad news?"

"Nothing really. Except that I ask you to pass on a favor to someone else, when you can."

The waitress brought out their orders and Hank didn't talk much. He didn't really know what to say. These people had taken care of him like he was part of their family. And the thought that he had forgotten Anne. Well, he just felt really bad.

The next morning, Hank got to the shop early to see if there was anything he could do to help Old Charlie out, like cleaning, organizing, answering the phone. At least there were no cats to take care of. He also called Matt to tell him he'd be on his way this afternoon. Probably would be there in time for dinner.

"Dad, that's great news."

"Matt, I need to ask you something."

"Sure, Dad. Anything."

"Why haven't I heard from Kate?"

"Well, she's kind of busy."

"Really?"

"Well, to be honest, she's a little disappointed you never called her back."

Hank didn't bother explaining that he thought Kate was going to call him. It didn't matter. He should have called her—it was just common sense—but there was nothing he could do about it now.

"I guess I did it again," admitted Hank.

"I'll talk to her. Don't worry. We'll have supper ready tonight. I'll leave work early to help her out. Just drive safe and keep me posted if anything comes up, okay?"

When Hank hung up the phone, he puttered around the shop, rehearsing in his mind what he would say to Kate when he saw her.

When the repairs were done and it was time to pay, Hank hoped that his credit card wasn't maxed out. Thankfully, it was approved. That would have been *really* embarrassing.

As he exited the shop, Hank texted Matt to let him know he was finally on his way. The drive to

Baltimore should be short and, hopefully, devoid of surprises.

He thought about Old Charlie's kindness, and how kindness could never be a liability when it came to doing good business. So, how could Hank pass on this goodwill to someone else? He thought about Dan. The kid who bought the van. Hank knew he wouldn't be able to pay for the unexpected transmission repair. And, it really wasn't his fault anyway. Fifteen hundred dollars would probably break the kid's bank account. That's when Hank decided that he would take the loss, pay for the repairs, and make one kid really happy. Actually, he had made two kids happy, when he counted giving his old truck to J.R. And now, he was hoping he could do something to make it up to a third kid, his only daughter, Kate.

Heading Home

When Hank put the key into the ignition, the old van fired right up. He could feel the humming of the engine, almost like a kitten purring. He hopped onto I-68, and felt energized. The skies were partly cloudy and it was in the 40s, so he didn't have to worry about snow. He cruised all the way to Hancock to catch I-70. He passed through Pecktonville, Big Pool, Clear Springs. Then the bigger cities of Hagerstown and Frederick without stopping for a coffee or donut. Why should he? The tank was half full and the van was running fine. Onward he zipped through New Market, Cookesville, and West Friendship.

Traffic started picking up as he neared Baltimore. Rush hour! Hank focused all of his energy on finding the beltway to swing around the south side of the city. *Where did all these lanes come from? And, all this traffic? Better pay close attention. No sense in getting into a fender bender this close to home.*

Then, there it was. Exactly as he remembered it. The Key Bridge. A quarter-mile truss bridge that spanned the Baltimore Harbor. Hank remembered when the bridge was being built during his college days. He never thought much about it back then, but today he viewed it as the engineering feat that it was, with its stately steel arch overlooking the Patapsco River. He had forgotten that it was a toll bridge, though. As he drove, he fumbled around for some quarters he had tucked away in the ashtray at the start of the trip. He hoped that no one, like Potter or Lucky, decided to treat themselves to a few. Ah, there they were!

$3.00? Highway robbery, he thought as he counted out the coins for the toll collector. As the van climbed toward the steel arch, Hank looked at the familiar Baltimore skyline. There was the old Legg Mason Building! And, the Baltimore Trust Building! On the other side of the bridge was the expansive Chesapeake Bay. Hank wasn't sure, but he thought he caught a glimpse of Rock Hall, his and Anne's favorite beach. His journey was finally over! Once he crossed the Patapsco, he'd be in Edgemere, where Kate and Matt lived.

Hank crossed the bridge and exited, turning onto North Point Drive. He thought it fitting that Kate lived near the place where his parents first met— at a dance hall at the Bay Shore Amusement Park, sometime back in the early '40s. He remembered how his parents never got over the fact that the park was bought out by Bethlehem Steel years before Hank was born. But in the late

'80s, that steelyard had been turned into a park by the State of Maryland. *How nice and convenient it would be to take his grandbaby fishing there, when he or she was old enough, of course.*

Hank's mind wandered between nostalgia and the future. When he "woke up", he found himself driving through North Point State Park. He quickly maneuvered a three-point turn to backtrack to Kate's house.

Blueberry Drive was a quaint seaside street lined with cozy pastel-painted cottages and the occasional white picket fence. There it was. 322. A bright yellow VW Bug was parked in the driveway. Hank parked across the street, turned the ignition off, and collapsed in his seat. He had made it. He was finally here. But, instead of feeling exuberated, he felt dog tired. He wanted to compose himself before knocking on the door. His mind was tingling and his limbs felt numb.

"Dad," called out Kate as she ran down the stoop and into the street. "Dad! Dad!"

Hank clambered out of the door with a smile as Kate threw her arms around him to welcome him home.

In that moment, all of the scenarios he had played in his mind about their first meeting were instantly erased. Here was his baby girl in his arms, and he could not say a thing. Not a *Hello, how are you.* Not *I'm sorry.* Not *I'm so glad to see you.* All of the feelings he had dreamed in his heart for so many years just poured out in tears. They trickled down his cheeks so he closed his eyelids, but they seeped out still.

During their reunion, a pickup truck drove by, and stopped abruptly. It was Matt. He looked the same to Hank, except that his face was a little fuller and he was growing a little scruff on his chin.

"Dad, you made great time," Matt said as he rolled down the window. "So good to see you!" Smiling, he pointed to a large brown paper bag on the front seat. "I hope you like Chinese food."

They walked into the little cottage, with Kate leading the way. Hank noticed that the exterior of the cottage was painted light blue with crisp, white trim. The last of the fall pansies colored the flowerbox under the front window with purples and yellows.

After dinner, Matt stoked a small fire in the cobblestone fireplace. They spent the rest of the evening having coffee with Hank retelling stories about his journey and Kate sharing her ultrasound photos of the baby. When it was time to sleep, Kate led Hank to the baby's nursery. It was a small room, with a white wooden crib, and an air mattress for Hank. "I hope you'll be comfortable here, Dad. Let me know if you need anything."

"I will. Thanks, Kate." Hank had wanted to speak with her alone. To tell her he was sorry. But, when he started to speak, she just put her finger on his lips.

"Tomorrow," Kate whispered. "I can help you take the van to its new owner. How does 10 o'clock sound?"

"I'll text Dan, but I think he has probably been more than ready for the last few weeks."

"Would you like something special for breakfast tomorrow, Dad?"

"How about if I help you make breakfast?"

The next morning, Hank got up early, found an iron frying pan, and started some bacon on the gas stove. Matt had gone off to work, and Kate had just come down the steps into the kitchen.

She was wearing a light blue sweater and jeans with her dark hair wrapped in a ponytail. She looked incredibly happy.

"Bacon is ready," Hank said proudly.

"How about some eggs to go with it?" Kate asked.

The two had a quiet breakfast. Hank made some coffee, and Kate asked him questions about the van. She wanted to know why he decided to make the trip all alone.

"It was something I guess I needed to do," he said. "Your mother and I had planned a road trip together. So..." Hank just shrugged his shoulders at his loss of explanation.

"I think I get that," she said with a slight smile.

"This young man, Dan. He lives in White Marsh," Hank said. "It's only about 20 minutes away. Let me give him a call and tell him we'll be on our way."

"I'll follow you in the Beetle."

"Kate, before we go," Hank put his hand on her forearm, "I need to tell you something."

"Sure, Dad. Is everything okay?"

"I don't know how to start." Hank closed his eyes for a moment. "Look, Kate. I'm so sorry that we, I mean, that I haven't been in touch with you. I'm sorry. I feel as if I've neglected you and…"

"Dad?"

"I mean, I didn't spend a lot of time with you during your teenage years…"

"Oh that. Yeah, I used to feel sad about it. I thought that once I was too big for you to carry me on your shoulders, you didn't maybe like being with me anymore. But now, in looking back at it, maybe that was immature of me to think that."

"No, Kate, it wasn't. I should have been there for you. I depended too much on your mother to do that for me."

"Dad…well, maybe I'm to blame, too."

"No, Kate. You're not to blame. Then, when your mom died, I became a bitter man. A man who lost his faith. His hope. Your mom would not have been happy with how I acted. I'm just blessed that my friend Joe put up with me all these years. And the guys too."

"Guys?"

"Oh, the guys in our old car club. We used to meet at the diner for breakfast a few times a week. It was they who suggested I sell the house and move out here."

There. He had finally said it.

"You sold the house?"

"Yes, I needed to leave Bakersfield. And, I needed to bring your mom back home. And, me too."

"Dad, I can't believe you're coming back for good."

"I've changed, Kate. Something happened to me on that road trip, too. I guess I got my faith in God back, and I've seen the good that people can do."

Kate, dumbfounded, didn't know what to say.

"What I'm saying is, what I'm asking is, is for you to forgive me."

"Oh, Dad. Okay, I do. I do forgive you. I hope you forgive me, too. I know I probably wasn't the best-behaved teenager."

"I love you, Kate."

"I love you, too, Dad. I do."

As Kate and Hank hugged, Hank wiped his eyes on his sleeve. "Guess we better get going to Dan's. He's probably thinking I may have changed my mind."

Kate laughed among sniffles. "I'm ready if you're ready."

As they got onto the beltway to head to White Marsh, Hank felt no remorse in handing the van over to Dan. In fact, after three weeks of driving, living, and eating in the van, he had felt as if he had become physically attached to the driver's seat. Now, he couldn't wait to hand over the keys to Dan.

Dan and his mother lived on Cape Lane, a bayside residential street that ran parallel to Bird River. Their house was a well-maintained one-story blonde brick ranch style. It was apparent that Dan's mother liked to garden, too. The yard was well-manicured. There was a winding, hand-laid stone path that invited guests to the front door. As Hank parked in the drive, he motioned to Kate to park and accompany him. But before they could ring the bell, Dan had already opened the garage door and come out to greet them.

"Mr. Hank?"

"You must be Dan."

They shook hands.

"It's a pleasure to meet you, sir."

"This is my daughter, Kate."

"Nice to meet you."

Even though the van had a little street salt sprayed on it, it looked better than Dan had ever imagined. Hank threw the young man the keys and now his mission was completed.

As Dan turned the ignition, Hank noticed a Kia Soul in the garage and a Honda Civic "Tuner". There was an older woman with arms crossed watching them from the front window, shaking her head in disapproval. Probably Dan's mother.

"It sounds great, Mr. Hank. Thank you so much for driving it out here. I really appreciate it. Would you and Kate like to come in for something to drink? I'd like to hear about your trip."

"Well, Kate, needs to get back home, and..."

"No, I don't, Dad. We'd love to," said Kate. "Dad's got a ton of stories from his odyssey across America in your van!"

Dan led the way through the front door. They were blasted by the cold reception from Dottie, his mother.

"Uh, mom. This is Mr. Hank, and his daughter, Kate. I've invited them in for coffee."

"Very well," she said sternly. "Have a seat."

As Dottie made the coffee, Dan listened to Hank intently about the little "tricks" he needed to know about the van, especially the window washer fix. Then, he broke the good news about the new engine and transmission.

"That's great," said Dottie with sarcasm in her voice. Perhaps she was hoping the van would just die, thought Hank. He couldn't figure out why she was so cold to Dan's idea of fixing up the van. Maybe it had to do with space in the garage?

"I shouldn't probably tell you this, but back in the day, me and my buddies, well, we used to street race back in Parkville. You know, to try and impress the girls!" Hank winked in Dan's direction.

"Dad!"

"Now, Kate, you didn't think your dad was an old nerd, did you? No harm was done. We were just a bunch of kids hanging out."

"Parkville? You didn't happen to know a guy named Doug Bryan, did you?" asked Dottie.

"Doug Bryan. Doug Bryan. Why, didn't he work at the old A&P grocery? Yeah, I think he was part of our crowd sometime. Why?"

"He's my brother. He started this whole annoying van club thing with my husband. Trying to relive old times. That's why Dan is such a fanatic."

"Aw, c'mon, Mom. I'm not a fanatic."

"Restoring that van isn't going to bring your dad back, son."

Dan rolled his eyes and ignored her. "Uncle Doug is gonna love this. Hey, Mr. Hank, do you want to come to the club sometime? We meet at the old Elks Hall third Saturday of the week. You can come too, Kate."

Now, Kate rolled her eyes. "I think I've had enough of old car clubs. That's how I spent my childhood. But, I'm sure my dad would love it."

Since Dottie seemed to be the town gossip, she wanted to know if they had any other mutual acquaintances. "Did you go to Parkville High School?"

"Yep, the good old black and gold."

"So did I."

"What year did you graduate?"

"1978."

"I was out of college a few years by then. I don't remember Doug having a little sister."

"Yeah, he used to bring all his buddies home. I had such a crush on Elliot White."

"Elliott? You mean the star football player from Overlea?"

"Yeah," sighed Dottie. "Sad thing, though. He ended up becoming a cop and got shot during a robbery a few years back."

"Sheesh."

Hank and Dottie reminisced for almost an hour. She filled him in on every one of her brother's friends who had stayed in the Baltimore area. She knew the whereabouts of some of those who had left, too. In an uncanny way, Dottie and Hank had a lot of mutual acquaintances.

"Funny, though, how I never met you," Hank said. "Did I ever come over to your house?"

"I think I remember you," Dottie said with a faint smile. "I think I maybe do."

Kate nudged her dad on the arm. "Dad, it's already noon. We should be going. Well, it was very nice meeting you both. Dottie, Dan, it was a pleasure."

"Maybe you can meet up with some of the old guys, Hank," Dottie said with a smile.

"I'd like that," Hank said.

As Kate and Hank got into the VW, Hank noticed that Dan was taking his mother by the hand, slowly walking her down the front steps to see his new ride. She didn't look quite as stern as she had before.

The fall passed into winter, and Thanksgiving felt like a real homecoming. Hank would be celebrating Christmas with family this year, which was surely going to be a blessing. On

Christmas Eve, the plan was to attend Kate and Matt's church, a Catholic church in the heart of Baltimore. Matt had a large, extended family and it was a tradition for all of them to celebrate Christmas Eve together. Hank now realized that his family had not dwindled down. No, it had grown exponentially. It was all in the way he chose to look at things.

The day before Christmas Eve, Dan called Hank to wish him Merry Christmas and to say thanks again for the van. He was sorry he hadn't called about the van club meetings, but he had been busy preparing the body of the van for paint and was redoing the interior. He wondered if Hank might like to see it. "And, my mom is also inviting you to church on Christmas Day. That is, if you'd like to come."

"Well, I'm going to church on Christmas Eve with the kids. But, I don't see why I can't go with you both on Christmas Day. So, yes, I'd love to."

When Hank arrived at the United Methodist Church, he found Dottie and Dan sitting in the second pew. He quietly entered and sat next to them. On the right side of the altar, an organist was triumphantly playing Christmas hymns. A tall, well-decorated Christmas tree sparkled on the left. Hank looked over at Dottie and smiled. This morning, she looked younger and light-hearted. The birth of the Lord can do that to a person.

The choir, dressed in royal blue robes, sang "O Come, All Ye Faithful." Dottie handed Hank a song book and he sang aloud to every Christmas carol. For Hank, the service was beautiful and the message about the Christ child meaningful. It brought back memories of days past when he attended Christmas service with his parents, grandparents, brothers, and sister. He really felt like he had come back home.

After the service, Dottie took Hank by the arm and introduced him to Pastor Rick. The young pastor was dressed in a white robe, with a long, red stole with two crosses on each end.

"Not to put Hank on the spot, but I think he would be perfect for the job, Pastor Rick."

"Job?"

Pastor Rick explained that their church needed a sexton. The church could supply a small salary and a mobile home on the church property in exchange for maintenance services. Would Hank be interested?

The old Hank would have been mortified to be put on the spot like that. And, he might have even metaphorically put Dottie on his blacklist. But, the old Hank didn't exist anymore. He had put his bitterness to rest somewhere along that long road between Bakersfield and Baltimore. The new Hank, now, was certainly interested.

A New Life

"You'll be there, won't you Mr. Hank?"

"What time?"

"Didn't you get Mom's message?"

"No, Dan. Sorry, I didn't."

"Well, she just wondered if you'd like to come over for lunch beforehand. She's making fried chicken and mashed potatoes."

"Two invitations in one week? That's a real treat. Sure. I'd love to."

Hank hung up the phone with a smile. Dan had been working on the old van since Christmas. Tomorrow was the sneak preview for Dan's closest friends, before it was presented at the old van club's 40th anniversary next Saturday.

Ever since Hank settled into his job as the new church sexton after Christmas, Dottie had been inviting him to dinner every week. It did take him some time to make the trailer feel like home, though. It was a rather small place, and even though he had sold or given away a lot of his furniture and belongings back in Bakersfield, he still couldn't fit everything he brought with him into the new place. The mobile home had only one small bedroom and a bathroom, an eat-in kitchen, and a small living room, but it was all Hank really needed. Dottie and the ladies from the church gave it a good cleaning before he moved in, and offered to help with a little decorating. Eventually, he felt at home in the place, but he didn't spend much time there. Between visiting Kate and Matt, and Dan and Dottie, and working at the church, he didn't have much time to sit around at home. Nor, did he cook much for himself either. His refrigerator was stocked with yogurt, cream for coffee, some eggs, cheese, and lunchmeat for quick meals. And, every Wednesday, one of the church ladies brought over a dish when they had their weekly prayer meetings.

Hank convinced the pastor that the church should open up a small thrift store to bring in money for the needy in the community. He was the first to make donations. A sofa and a chair, some end tables, a few knickknacks, books, and the like. He bought a 2000 Ford Escape, so he could do pick-ups and deliveries. Shorty would surely be proud.

Hank had grown pleasingly accustomed to the weekly dinners at Dan's and Dottie's, too. Dottie sure could cook, and this also gave Hank the chance to see the progress Dan was making on the van. The kid had recruited three of his friends to help him with the work. And, when they couldn't do the work themselves, they asked the old school guys in the car club for advice.

One of those guys, Tom, had a local shop, reminiscent of Potter's old place with its muscle cars. Tom told the kids he'd help with the repairs if the young people watched, learned, and helped out. It was all part of a foundation that Tom had formed with his friends, the mission of which was to introduce the old car hobby to the next generation, and to hopefully develop within them a lifelong interest in fixing up these old cars. Even Dottie came around to Tom's shop once or twice, just to see what all the hype was about.

Hank was surprised that Dan's friends took such an interest in the old van. He figured that the younger crowd wouldn't be interested in learning about vehicles from "grandpa's era". He thought they'd be more intrigued with those Honda and Subaru "Tuners" with their "fart" pipes, or one of those big F-350 Diesels, belching out all that black smoke. Somehow this old van, which had been mocked and hated, was now linking the generations together.

When Dan told Hank that Dottie left a message, he was surprised. He didn't remember getting a voicemail. He rarely checked his messages anyway. Occasionally, he and Joe called one another to catch up. Hank just thought it was easier to text when they couldn't reach each other. Imagine that.

He punched the "one" key to review his messages. Sure enough, Dottie's message was there. Hank sometimes wondered if she was interested in being anything more than friends, but when it came to women, he felt pretty clueless. It had been so long since he had dated anyone. Like 40 years long. Dottie's voice sounded gentle and kind, nothing like the woman he had met four months ago. He deleted the message, and found another one hidden there. From a number he didn't recognize.

"Hank, how are you? Bella Vista hasn't been the same without you. Did you make it to Baltimore okay? How are Kate and Matt? Call me back and let me know you got there, ok? I've got some news to tell you."

How could he have forgotten about Shirley?

He replayed the message and listened to the voicemail again. The recording said that she had called in December. Almost three months ago. He felt like a horrible friend.

Should he call her back? What was the news she had to tell him?

He accidentally hit redial and her phone started ringing.

"You've reached Shirley. Sorry I can't take your call right now. Leave your name and number and I'll call you back. Have a blessed day." It beeped. Should he leave a message? She'd know that he had called.

"Shirley, Hi. Uh, this is Hank? Um, Sorry I haven't called you. I just got...your message now. Today. I got here okay. I'm fine. Kate's fine. Well, I've been really busy and well, anyway..." The voicemail cut him off. He had no idea if his message had been recorded. He certainly hoped not.

The clock on the phone said 3 p.m. so he drove over to Kate's. The house was quiet when he walked in. Maybe she was taking a nap.

"Dad?"

"Yeah, honey. Are you okay?"

"I'll be right down."

Kate looked radiant and tired at the same time. She also looked ready to deliver a baby. She still had another couple of weeks to go.

"Dad, that look on your face. What's wrong?"

Hank told Kate about Shirley. And how at first he had been leery of her because she was a biker girl. He told her about Willard's last meal and all the mysterious histories from different sources— Joe, the truckers, the gals at the diner—that no one wanted to share with him. He suspected that Shirley was linked to that fatal day somehow but he didn't know how. All he knew was that Miss Myrtle, the old widow lady, had taken her in as a teenager. But, the worst thing, out of all of this, is that she had called in December and he never returned her call. He should have called her to let her and the folks in Bella Vista know that he had gotten there safely. How could he have forgotten?

"Dad, you were so wiped out when you got here. You'd gone through so much. Then there were the holidays, then you moved and settled into your new job, looked for a new car. You've been busy."

"Those are just excuses, Kate. The hard thing is owning up to how stupid I was."

"Well, did you call her back?"

"Yeah. Accidentally. I hit redial and left a terrible message."

"Dad, what's gotten into you? If she's your friend, she'll understand. Just call her back."

"Should I?"

"Yes."

Okay, if Kate says I should call her back, I will. Hank started to blush.

"Dad, what's going on?"

Hank didn't know how to answer that question. The only woman he had ever talked to Kate about was Anne. It felt awkward.

"Dad, it's okay. Mom wouldn't want you to be sad and alone."

"It's not that, Kate. Shirley was...is a very nice lady. But she's in Bella Vista and I'm here. But, now that you've brought it up. I was wondering what you thought of...well, how *would* I know if a woman is interested? I mean..."

"Dad, if you're talking about Dottie. Yes, I think she is. She invites you to dinner every week. That's very nice of her. But a lady won't do that if she's not interested."

Hank blushed again. "You mean she's not inviting me because she feels sorry for me?"

Kate shook her head "no".

"Well, she did invite me to lunch tomorrow. Dan and his friends are going to show off all the work they did on the van for me and Dottie."

"Dad, that's great. Just go, and have a good time. That's all you need to do."

The next day Hank worked at the church in the morning, took a shower, put on his best shirt, and even wore some cologne. Hank brought some flowers for Dottie. And, as usual, the meal was spectacular.

"Mom, that was the best lunch I've ever had," said Dan. "You sit and relax and we'll all clean up. Then, we'll take you and Hank for a ride."

Dan and his friends—two young men and a nice girl named Sally—cleaned up the kitchen with lightning speed, so fast that Dottie and Hank could barely finish their coffee. After Dottie did her inspection of the kitchen, Dan told everyone to meet him in the front yard. "Give me just a minute," he said.

The garage door opened and the van made its appearance. There were no boxes to move out of the way, no jumper cables, no rope to pull it outside. Dan turned the key and the van fired right up. *That kid must have done some custom exhaust work 'cause she sounded great,* Hank thought.

Dan rolled the van slowly outside into the sunlight, the red paint glistening. Dan had gone with vintage wheels and some pin striping to finish out the exterior. It looked absolutely amazing!

Hank felt a tear forming in his eye. He remembered the day when he and Anne had decided to buy that old van, despite how "rustic" it looked. They smiled silently at one another as they signed the paperwork at the used car dealership. They each knew what the other was thinking.

"You've got to check out the engine, Mr. Hank. Come here."

Dan got out of the van and popped the hood. The engine looked almost brand new. There was not a spec of dirt or oil on it. "It took me months to get it off, but I did it."

"It looks fantastic, Dan. You did a great job."

"Ok, everybody in! We're going cruising." Dan helped Dottie into the front seat as Dan's friends scrambled into the back with Hank slowly following.

"These leather seats make it feel like a luxury van," Hank said.

"So you like them?" Sally asked. "We felt we'd go for luxury and comfort over the retro look. So, glad you like it." Hank agreed that the new seats, headliner, and carpeting were definitely much nicer than the old shag carpeted interior and cracked vinyl seats.

"It even has air conditioning," said Dan. "And I fixed the windshield washer."

Dan drove up Ebenezer Road, then Eastern Avenue towards Edgemere, where Kate and Matt lived. The ride was smooth. All of Hank's high school and college memories rolled back into his mind, like an old home movie.

"Mom, you haven't said a word," Dan said. "What do you think?"

"I'm so proud of you, son," she said. "You've done an incredible job."

Hank could tell from the inflections in her voice that she was beaming with motherly pride. "But, you couldn't have done it without Hank. Thanks, Hank, for helping Dan live out his dream of honoring his dad."

Hank choked up. He couldn't speak.

"Does that mean you'll come to our anniversary celebration next week?" Dan asked.

"Of course, I'll be there. I'm making the food, aren't I?"

The ride was sweet and dream-like. It had all been a dream for Dan, for Dottie, for Hank, and Dan's young friends, all touched in different ways. The young people all chatted in the back about how they thought it was cool that the van was a mix of old and new.

But, Hank knew that it was more than a refurbishing job. The old van was brought back to life, the very heart and soul of it restored! Through a loving and collaborative effort of folks from around the country who didn't even know one another. It started with Hank and Anne, then Joe and J.R., Potter—in an obtuse way—Old Charlie at the Little Hurtin' Campgrounds, Lucky—although inadvertently—Mike and the guys at the car club in Bella Vista, Joe (again) and Mr. Lujan, the cowboy kid in Oklahoma, the folks at the Ohio car cruise who appreciated the van for what she was, the second "Old Charlie" in Cumberland, and Tom and the guys in the Baltimore car club.

Each of them had a hand in transforming the van into something more than metal and wheels. It was about teamwork, about love and caring, about building on dreams, and giving back to your fellow man. Dan had put on the amazing finishing touches and Dottie gave it the final blessing. What a beautiful testament to Dan's dad and Dottie's husband.

Hank sensed that Anne was part of it, too, and hoped somehow that she was looking down on them, happy that they could help the kid realize his dream.

Then, Hank's phone rang.

"Dad. It's Matt. I'm taking Kate to the hospital. I'd pick you up but there's no time. No time. Can you meet us there?"

"She's not due for a few weeks. What's wrong? Is she okay?"

"Her water broke. So, the doctor said the baby will be have to be born today, or tomorrow at the latest. Gotta go. Oh yeah, we're on our way to Franklin Square Hospital. Gotta go."

Dan offered to drive Hank to the hospital. "I can drop you guys off at the house. It shouldn't take too long, Hank." No, everyone enthusiastically jumped on going along...to keep Hank company.

"It's nice of you to come with me, but I don't expect you all to wait here all night," Hank said once they got to the hospital.

Everyone insisted on waiting with Hank until the baby was born. Matt rushed into the waiting room to see if Hank had made it there. "Matt, sit right down with us and let me introduce you to everybody," Hank said.

"Hank, dads go in the delivery room nowadays," said Dottie.

"They do?"

"Yes, they do. I gotta get back to Kate, Dad. I'll keep you posted."

They waited for hours, Dan heading to the cafeteria to bring everyone coffee and donuts. They all took turn telling stories and, of course, Dottie had to jokingly tell everyone how uncooperative Dan had been from the moment of his birth.

"He was so comfortable, he didn't want to come out. They had to pull him out with forceps."

"Well, that explains the shape of his head," jabbed Peter, one of the trio. Everybody laughed as Dan threw a few fake punches at the perpetrator.

At about midnight, Hank started dozing. Dottie too. With their heads bobbing and weaving, Dan and his friends talked quietly and changed the channel on the waiting room T.V. to watch the late night shows.

Around 3 a.m., a nurse found everyone sleeping. She gently nudged Hank to tell him that the baby had been born and that Kate was doing fine. He could see her in a little bit. "She's 8 pounds even. She's a good crier too."

Hank was overjoyed. He felt like the happiest man alive. In his heart, he knew that Joe and the guys at the diner had done a good deed by nudging him to move to Baltimore. What would it have been like to hear this good news in Bakersfield, so far away? He was here. In the now. And he was soon going to meet his granddaughter. He would teach her everything he knew about cars and fishing and camping and…. Everyone got up and hugged Hank. Dottie kissed him on the cheek. "Congratulations, Grandpa Hank."

Walking into Kate's room, Hank's legs felt wobbly. *I'm a grandpa.* It was a huge responsibility, and he was going to make sure that he did everything he could to make sure that his grandbaby grew up right.

As he walked through the door, he saw an exhausted but elated Kate, and Matt, the proud dad, who couldn't take his eyes off of the baby. She was wrapped in a pink hospital blanket. All Hank could see was a little round red face and a mass of black hair.

"Dad," Kate said sleepily. "Meet Joy Anne, your granddaughter."

Hank was speechless. But he knew what he felt. He felt that his heart had finally opened up and was ready to love deeply again. He hadn't realized how much he had closed it. And, now, with the birth of Joy Anne, the floodgates had been completely opened.

A Final Good Bye to Anne

Anne's memorial service was set for the Tuesday after Memorial Day. It would take place at Rock Hall, the small bayside town where Anne was born. It was planned for 10 a.m. sharp. Hank was getting ready, combing his hair, putting on a little cologne, and tucking in his shirt. He picked up the beautiful urn from the shelf and felt a sharp pain in his heart as he placed it back into its blue marble case. So snuggly it fit. Like it belonged there. "This is it, Annie," he said as the lid flipped shut. The feelings were still there. They just weren't as painful.

There had been a slight adjustment to the plans for the memorial service. When Hank found out that it was prohibited to scatter ashes on any beach in the bay, he felt his heart drop to his knees. This was Anne's last wish, and now he could not fulfill it.

Troubled about the news, Hank confided in Dottie at dinner one night. What if they planted a small memorial garden on the grounds near the church cemetery, suggested Dottie. Perhaps they could bury Anne's ashes there. It could be a private place for Hank to sit and ponder and pray. She could plant some flowers and an herb garden in the summer, or maybe a tree on the spot where Anne would be put to rest.

"Would a red maple sapling be a suitable memorial tree?"

"Yes. Absolutely wonderful." Hank said, thankful for Dottie's suggestions.

Dottie and Hank began working on the garden. They covered a 10-foot by 10-foot square with old newspapers to kill the grass, then laid down compost from the church kitchen on top. Once the grass was dead, Hank cut out the sod and turned it onto its back then mixed it into the sandy loam. After the last frost, Dottie scattered seeds for black-eyed susans and purple cone flowers, and she planted some geraniums and petunias and impatiens. She monitored the garden religiously, and when the weather warmed, she would plant herbs, like basil, cilantro, and rosemary. The church asked for donations to purchase a white marble bench for the garden, and Hank filled in the walkway he had dug with irregularly-shaped sandstone and slate. By Memorial Day, the garden would flourish as a source of beauty and inspiration.

To get to the memorial service, Hank, Kate, Matt, and baby Joy Anne would travel by boat from

Edgemere to Rock Hall captained by Matt's best friend, Jack. The ride would take thirty minutes. Once they arrived at the slip, Dan would pick them up in the van and take them to the beach where the memorial service would take place. It would be a small, intimate service, with Pastor Rick presiding, and Matt's family, Dottie and Dan, in attendance. Hank invited the small group, as well as many of the parishioners, to meet them for dinner and fellowship at the church later in the day.

"Kate, are you all ready to go?" Hank asked, as he walked through the front door of their bayside cottage. He looked in the hall mirror, combed his hair one last time, and put on the jacket he had slung over his shoulder. He felt nervous.

As Hank, Kate, and Matt with baby Joy Anne in tow, walked across the street to the dock, a sleek Sea Ray cruiser pulled up. Matt helped Kate put the infant life jacket on Joy Anne as she squirmed and squealed. Hank noticed that the cruiser was named "Happy Daze."

No way. He smiled to himself, thinking how God's goodness had a hand in their plan. Hank sure wished that Joe and some of the guys from the diner could have been here to see that! They sat on the back seat of the boat facing the rippling waves as the cruiser picked up speed.

The ride to Rock Hall was calm and smooth and uneventful. It was a beautiful day, sunny, with few lone, floating clouds.

When they got to the slip, Matt helped Kate off of the boat, while Hank held a squirming Joy Anne. After Hank handed the baby to her mother, he looked at the parking lot, expecting to see the van. But, no one was there. He was just about to pull out his cell phone when a sharp, black Chevy Suburban pulled up. A young man in a dress shirt, nice slacks, and a tie jumped out.

"Uncle Hank, so good to see you." Hank ran up to the driver's side to give the young man a hug.

"J.R.? What a surprise. Where's your dad?"

"Look behind you," he said.

"Hank, so good to see you, pal," he said as he hopped out of the truck. "So glad you're still in one piece, too." Hank's heart was racing.

"Joe, I don't know what to say. It's so great that you made the trip to come out here. But how did you know we'd be at the boat slip?"

"You're talking to Joe, here, Hank. Haven't you learned anything?"

Hank introduced Joe and J.R. to Kate and Matt. "And this is Joy Anne," said Hank proudly. "Say hi to Uncle Joe, Joy Anne."

"Aahhhhooooo," she gurgled.

Joe smiled at Joy Anne and started to play peek-a-boo.

"Pretty nice wheels, J.R.," said Hank reminding them they better get to the beach.

"It's a rental, Uncle Hank. Why not go to this important day in style?"

As everyone hopped in the truck, Hank saw that there was an infant car seat in the back for the baby. "You guys sure thought of everything," said Hank. The beach was only a five-minute drive away, but the two-lane coastal road was starting to get clogged up with traffic.

"It's not usually this crowded on a week day, is it, Kate?" asked Hank.

"No, Dad. It's usually pretty quiet here, especially until the kids get out of school."

"Don't worry, Hank. We'll drop you off and go find a place to park. It'll be okay," Joe said in a calm manner.

As the Suburban pulled up to the beach, Hank began to recognize a few of the parked cars. There's the van, and Pastor Rick's SUV. And, Tom's cool old Corvair.

Pastor Rick asked Hank if he was ready to begin. Hank nodded in approval and the good pastor quietly motioned the family and friends to congregate for the memorial service.

"Brothers and sisters. Thank you all for coming all the way here today, to Rock Hall, the birthplace of a woman named of Anne Johnson. I didn't have the pleasure of knowing Anne personally, but I do know her husband, Hank, who is with us here today. And Hank and Anne's daughter, Kate, and her family.

What I know about Anne is that she was a loving wife and mother. She and Hank met in college and soon after, they became inseparable. They graduated college and two years later, they were married. They always talked about traveling the country, making a road trip, but they never did. They both started working, and then Kate was born. But, when Kate was nine years old, Hank got offered a job in California, and so they made the trip and they stayed. Away from family and friends and connections and ties. But, Hank and Anne and Kate made new friends and found a church home there. Anne and Hank started helping with the youth group, so Kate could connect with others her age, and continued on even after Kate got older. They went to church every Sunday, helped at fundraisers, and were active in their community.

Then, Kate moved back to Baltimore to go to college. Empty nesters, Anne and Hank started creating new dreams. They found an old Dodge van, and bought it, with the hopes of refurbishing it and taking it on a cross-country road trip. But, then, soon after, Anne became ill. She had her good days and bad, but she rarely complained. She put her faith in the Lord for healing. And, when He called her home, she went peacefully.

Hank finally did make that trip cross-country a few months ago to bring his beloved Anne back to her final resting place, the place of her birth, right here in Rock Hall. For that, we can be truly thankful. Lastly, I would like to add that Hank has become a wonderful addition to our church community as our sexton. Brothers and sisters, know that, even though we grieve the loss of

Anne, we can also take comfort that she is now with the Lord, in peace and in rest."

Kate squeezed Hank's arm and passed baby Joy Anne to her grandfather. The little infant cooed, "Mamaaaaoooo."

Kate grabbed a tissue and wiped the corner of her eye, and laughed with tears at the antics of baby Joy Anne. She rose and slowly took her place to speak to the small crowd.

"It has been five years since my mother, Anne Johnson, passed away, and I still miss her. I know that my daughter Joy Anne will never have the chance to meet her in this life, but I am comforted by the fact that my mom is in a better place, surrounded by the Lord and his angels."

"Maaaaaaaaaaaa," Joy Anne babbled. Hank bounced the baby on his knee to quiet her.

"When my mom died," Kate continued. "I wrote a poem for her, a poem I never shared with anyone. But, this week, I have rewritten that poem and would like to share this newer version with you all here today."

Restored in Heart & Soul
By Kate Manchielli

Five years ago my mother left this world,

I felt such sorrow all I did was cry.

My life once secure now became unfurled,

For I never thought she could ever die.

I felt as if I lost my father, too,

I felt like an orphan, no place to go.

Dad wouldn't talk or say his feelings true,

His heart bled a sadness I could not know.

Across the country, alone he did roam

In his van, through mountains, deserts, or a country road.

Now he has come back to his childhood home

With seeds of love and faith in his heart, sewed.

Loving memories of my mother Anne,

Are all we have, for she's gone to the Lord.

To peace and goodness as 'fore the world began

Is what we all need to be working toward.

Tears and sadness and grieving take their toll,

But, with God's love, we are restored, in heart and soul.

After the service, Hank's friends offered many kind words and comforting hugs. Hank thanked Pastor Rick for making the long drive to Rock Hall so that Anne's final wishes could be fulfilled. After everyone left the beachside, Hank took one last look, then climbed in the Suburban to take the boat back to Edgemere.

The church grounds were quiet and empty when Hank and his family arrived. Matt took baby Joy Anne for a stroll, while Hank spent some time with Kate in the memorial garden. He set the blue marble box on the bench, near the spot where it would be buried later in the day, along with the red maple sapling as a memorial. It was quiet and sunny, and there was a gentle wind.

"Dad, it's quite beautiful. You've done a wonderful job."

Hank took Kate's hand as they looked at the garden, spending the time in prayer and memory.

As the guests began to arrive, Joe approached the two quietly. He tapped Hank on the shoulder and handed him a crisp, white envelope. "One of your friends who couldn't be here today asked me to give his to you." Joe patted Hank on the shoulder and walked back to the church.

Hank opened the envelope to find within it a handwritten letter.

Dear Hank,

I'm so glad to hear that you are okay. We were all so very worried about you. Then, I remembered that Mike from the car club had gotten a telephone call from a Mr. Lujan, who sent the parts so you could get the engine fixed. Mike still had his number in his phone, so we called him and found out that he was friends with your friend, Joe back in Bakersfield. Mr. Lujan gave us Joe's phone number, and so that's how we found out you were okay.

By now, your grandchild has been growing. I heard that it was a girl, but I forgot to ask what her name was. I wish many blessings to your grandbaby for a happy and full life. I also pray that the memorial service for Anne will be a comfort to you.

I never had a chance to tell you this, but I wanted to let you know, Hank, how much you have impacted my life. You were such a kind friend to me. It was nice just being able to talk to you. I guess I never had a chance to tell you how much it meant to me.

When I learned you were on a cross country road trip, I was amazed. Amazed at the bravery you had to step out of your comfort zone and make a long trip through parts unknown. I too was making such a trip when I was a teen. But, instead of running to something, like you were. I was running away. Trying to escape from my father, who hung around with a bad crowd. I won't go into details, but I will say that he was hell bent on finding me and bringing me back home. He traced me to Bella Vista. How? I don't know. What I do know was by the time he got there, he had run out of money. He was a smooth talker, he never hurt no one, that is, until he decided to steal some cash from that diner where you liked to eat breakfast. They called the Sherriff on him, but instead of giving himself up, he ran toward the Sherriff with a gun in his hand and he got

shot. I'll never figure out why he did that.
My dad suffered for days in the hospital
before he died. When I visited him, he told
me he was sorry. I could forgive him, but I
couldn't forgive myself. I felt like a rotten
apple fallen off of a bad tree. If I wouldn't
have run away, then maybe my dad wouldn't
have died. That's when Miss Myrtle took
me in. I blamed myself for a long time. I
stayed in that town to try and leave a good
mark on it instead of a bad one like my dad.

Anyway, that's all in the past now, but I
wanted you to know. The funny thing is that
I was on my way to California when I ran
out of money in Bella Vista. You know how
that is. ☺ You got stuck there, too.
Maybe Bella Vista is like a tollhouse for
tired souls. And, you leave when you are
ready. Anyway, I'm writing you this letter
from the road. I'm heading to California and
not sure where I'll set myself down but I'm
enjoying the ride. In a way, I'm finally
finishing the road trip I set out to do
twenty-five years ago. You were my

inspiration, the one who nudged me to leave Bella Vista in your own way, and to move on to where I was first headed. Anyway, if I don't hear from you again, know that you have a friend on the west coast. And that you'll always be in my thoughts and prayers.

Love, Shirley Willard
April 2, 2016

It was difficult for Hank to hold back the emotions that this letter stirred, emotions hidden deeply within his being. Emotions of sadness, emotions of shame, and, especially, emotions of regret. If it weren't for Kate, he would have broken down and let out the sobs that welled-up inside.

"Who's the letter from, Dad?" Kate asked when she saw the expression on her dad's face.

"From a treasure of a friend," Hank said with a sniffle. "A treasure I don't really deserve."

Dottie motioned for everyone to come inside the church and have dinner.

"You go in, Kate. I'll be there in a minute."

Hank lingered in the little memorial garden to think. Shirley had only kind words to say about him when he had forgotten all about her. He had judged her from the beginning, and didn't want to even talk to her at first. But, she only saw in her own soul the things she needed to work on while recognizing all the good that was in him. He was joyful that she had made peace in her heart.

He bowed his head and took one last moment to reflect on Anne. He took a deep breath and exhaled.

He stood up and straightened his coat. He felt lighter, knowing that she was back home. He thought about his love for her, those early years, their wedding day, the day Kate was born, the move to Bakersfield, and he reflected on how life continued on...even without her.

"Anne, this is it. You can rest now. Peace be to you, dear."

Hank looked up and could see Dottie watching him from afar. He motioned to her to come to the garden. She looked lovely in her flowing dress as she walked toward him.

"What is it, Hank?" Dottie said softly as she approached him.

"I just wanted to say...thank you, Dottie," said Hank.

"Why, Hank. You're so very welcome."

"Thank you for everything, Dottie. For everything."

Together, they looked upon the small memorial park, which they had nurtured with their own hands. "We probably should go," said Hank as he extended his arm to her. "It sure is a pretty, peaceful day, isn't it, Dottie?"

"It sure is, Hank. It sure is."

The End

About the Author

Dave Bielecki is the publisher of *Car Show & Cruise Guide* (www.carcruiseguide.com) and *Upper Bay Boating* (www.upperbayboating.com) and is the Executive Director of the Custom and Classic Car Educational Foundation (www.savethehobby.org), the mission of which is "to promote the custom and classic car culture and history to the public, along with encouraging a new generation of enthusiasts."

In *Restored Heart & Soul*, Mr. Bielecki's first book, he combines his love of classic cars with a desire to invite others to revisit their relationship with God.

Mr. Bielecki currently resides with his wife, Diane, his son, Daniel, their two cats and a few classic cars in various stages of being restored, heart and soul.

CPSIA information can be obtained
at www.ICGtesting.com
Printed in the USA
BVOW03s2157271016
466169BV00004B/9/P

9 780997 772708